HANDBOOK OF
INTERNATIONAL ACCOUNTING

SUBSCRIPTION NOTICE

This Wiley product is updated on a periodic basis with supplements to reflect important changes in the subject matter. If you purchased this product directly from John Wiley & Sons, Inc., we have already recorded your subscription for this update service.

If, however, you purchased this product from a bookstore and wish to receive (1) the current update at no additional charge, and (2) future updates and revised or related volumes billed separately with a 30-day examination review, please send your name, company name (if applicable), address, and the title of the product to:

Supplement Department
John Wiley & Sons, Inc.
One Wiley Drive
Somerset, NJ 08875
1-800-225-5945

For customers outside the United States, please contact the Wiley office nearest you:

Professional & Reference Division
John Wiley & Sons Canada, Ltd.
22 Worcester Road
Rexdale, Ontario M9W 1L1
CANADA
(416) 236-3580
1-800-263-1590
FAX 1-800-675-6599

John Wiley & Sons, Ltd.
Baffins Lane
Chichester
West Sussex, PO19 1UD
UNITED KINGDOM
(44) (243) 779777

Jacaranda Wiley Ltd.
PRT Division
P.O. Box 174
North Ryde, NSW 2113
AUSTRALIA
(02) 805-1100
FAX (02) 805-1597

John Wiley & Sons (SEA) Pte. Ltd.
37 Jalan Pemimpin
Block B # 05-04
Union Industrial Building
SINGAPORE 2057
(65) 258-1157

HANDBOOK OF INTERNATIONAL ACCOUNTING

1994 Cumulative Supplement

Edited by

FREDERICK D.S. CHOI

Leonard N. Stern School of Business, New York University

JOHN WILEY & SONS, INC.

New York • Chichester • Brisbane • Toronto • Singapore

Library of Congress Cataloging in Publication Data:

Handbook of international accounting / edited by Frederick D.S. Choi
    p. cm.
    Kept up to date with annual supplements.
    Includes bibliographical references.
    ISBN 0-471-51487-X (cloth)
    ISBN 0-471-30395-X (supplement)
    1. International business enterprises—Accounting.
  2. International business enterprises—Accounting—Standards.
  3. Comparative accounting. I. Choi, Frederick D. S., 1942– .
  HF5686.I56H36   1991
  657'.96—dc20   91-16011

Printed in the United States of America

10 9 8 7 6 5 4 3 2 1

CONTRIBUTORS

Page ix, replace entry for Roy A. Chandler *with:*

Roy A. Chandler, FCA, is a lecturer in accounting and a Coopers & Lybrand fellow at Cardiff Business School, University of Wales College of Cardiff. He is a former secretary to the International Auditing Practices Committee of IFAC. He has written many articles in professional and academic journals.

Page ix, replace first two lines of entry for Anthony M. Dalessio *with:*

Anthony N. Dalessio, CPA, is the deputy director general of the International Federation of Accountants.

Gunter Dufey, DBA, is professor of international business and finance at the Graduate School of Business Administration, The University of Michigan. His academic interests center on international money and capital markets, as well as financial policy of multinational corporations. He currently serves as a consultant to a number of international companies and is both a prolific author and a frequent lecturer.

Page x, replace first sentence in entry for David K. Eiteman *with:*

David K. Eiteman, PhD, has retired as professor of international finance at the John E. Anderson Graduate School of Management, UCLA. He is a visiting professor in the School of Business at the Hong Kong University School of Science and Technology.

Page x, add after entry for David K. Eiteman:

Ian H. Giddy, PhD, MBA, is a research fellow at the New York University Salomon Center. He has also served as director of the International Product Group at Drexel Burnham Lambert and consultant to a number of multinational corporations and financial institutions. He is the author of several books and numerous articles on international finance, financial markets, and risk management.

Page xi, replace first sentence in entry for Frank J. Maurer *with:*

Frank J. Maurer, CPA, is director of internal audit for United Hospitals Medical Center in Newark, New Jersey. A research-oriented CPA, with degrees in Economics and Accounting, he has also worked for Deloitte & Touche in New York City and for Pace University, where he taught economics.

Page xii, replace entry for Robert Sempier *with:*

Robert Sempier, CPA, is the former executive director of the International Federation of Accountants, an organization comprising 106 professional accountancy bodies from 78 countries.

Page xiii, add after entry for Rebecca Todd*:*

Jon Turner, PhD, is director of the Center for Research on Information Systems at New York University. His most recent research includes studies of interorganizational systems and new forms of organizing work that take advantage of technology. For the past six months he has been visiting professor at the Copenhagen Business School. He received his Ph. D. and his M.S. from Columbia University and his B.E. from Yale University.

Norman R. Walker is a partner and currently regional managing partner of Law Firm and Law Department Services for Price Waterhouse. He is a former director of MNC Client Services for Price Waterhouse World Firm. Mr. Walker is president of the Price Waterhouse Foundation; officer and trustee of the University of Oregon Foundation; vice president of the International Accounting Section of the American Accounting Association; and co-author of the Price Waterhouse Audit Guidance Series.

PREFACE

The *Handbook of International Accounting* continues to serve as a practical reference for financial managers, credit and security analysts, professional accountants and auditors, bankers, lawyers, and those whose responsibilities span the international dimensions of reporting and control. In keeping with the Wiley tradition, this supplement (1) updates existing chapters with a major addition to Chapter 19 by James Ratliff to include a new section on accounting for postretirement benefits other than pensions, and (2) expands the *Handbook's* topical coverage to include a chapter on external auditing. Authored by Norman R. Walker of Price Waterhouse, the chapter provides valuable insights on how to manage the ongoing relationship with external auditors. Written from a practicing accountant's perspective, the chapter's contents should prove helpful to financial managers of multinational companies, as well as those who must engage the services of an external auditor for statutory, due diligence, or financial control purposes.

We wish to thank our contributors for their continued support in this award-winning effort. We also welcome Norman Walker to this group of distinguished contributors.

New York, New York   FREDERICK D.S. CHOI
January 1994

SUPPLEMENT CONTENTS

Note to the Reader: Materials new to *this* supplement are indicated by an asterisk (*) in the left margin of the contents listed below and throughout the supplement. Sections not in the main bound volume are indicated by a (New) after the title.

CHAPTER 2

INTEGRATION OF WORLD FINANCIAL MARKETS—PAST, PRESENT, AND FUTURE

Roy C. Smith

New York University and Goldman, Sachs & Co.

SUPPLEMENT CONTENTS

2.3 GLOBALIZATION IN THE 1980s.

Page 2 · 8, replace Exhibit 2.1 with:

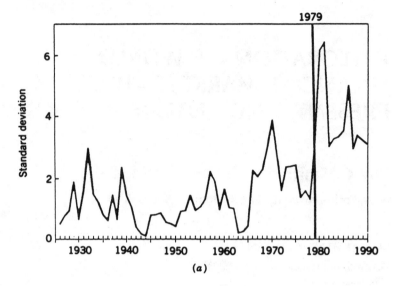

Note: In this chart, volatility is measured by the annual standard deviation of monthly returns of a 20-year Treasury bond index.

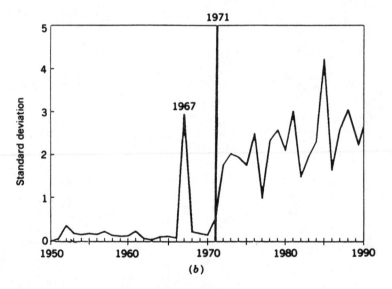

Note: In this chart, volatility is measured by the annual standard deviation of monthly percentage changes in the nominal U.S. dollar/pound sterling exchange rate.

Exhibit 2.1.   Exchange rate and interest rate volatility. (a) Volatility of Treasury bond yields, 1926–1990 (b) Volatility of the dollar/pound exchange rate, 1950–1990. *Source:* **Board of Governors, Financial Markets section.**

Page 2 • 10, replace Exhibit 2.2 with:

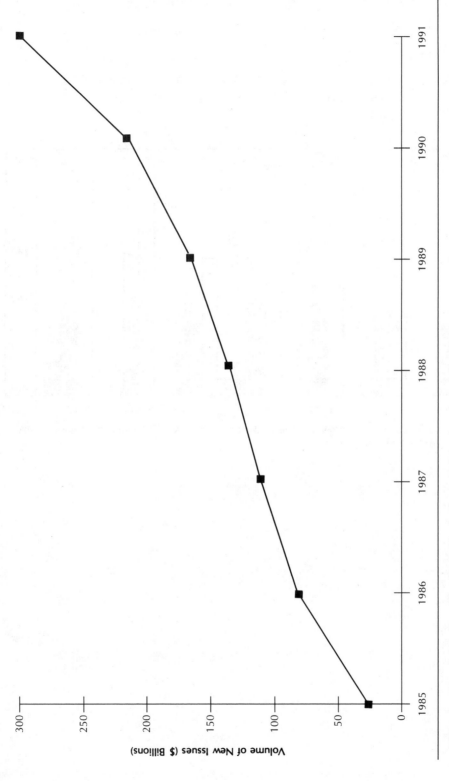

Exhibit 2.2. Growth in collateralized securities in the United States. *Source:* Securities Data Corporation.

Page 2 · 11, replace Exhibit 2.3 with:

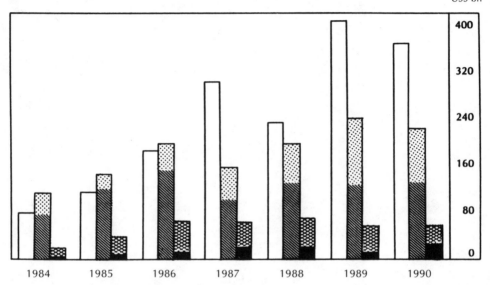

Net new international bank lending

Gross bond issues

} Net new bond financing

Gross new Euronote facilities

} Net new Euronote placements

Exhibit 2.3. Activity in international financial markets. *Sources:* **BIS data and estimates, Bank of England, AIBD, and Euroclear.**

Page 2 · 12, replace Exhibit 2.4 with:

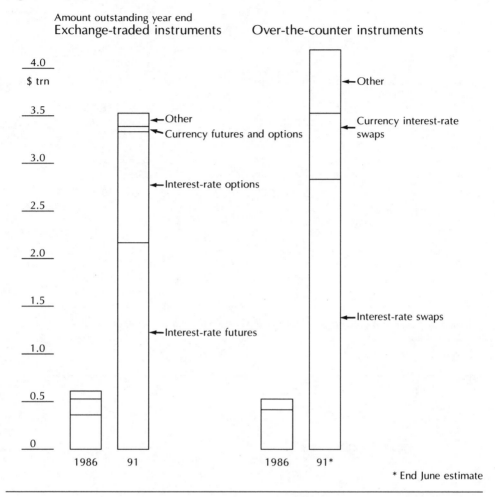

Exhibit 2.4.   **Exchange-traded and OTC derivatives outstanding, End–1991.** *Source:* **BIS.**

Page 2 · 12, replace Exhibit 2.5 with:

	Announced Gross New Issues				Net New Issues				Stocks at end-1990
	1987	1988	1989	1990	1987	1988	1989	1990	1990
				in billions of US dollars					
Straight fixed-rate issues	120.4	160.8	149.5	166.5	68.0	99.0	89.0	80.7	1,008.1
US dollar	*29.4*	*47.3*	*54.6*	*52.9*	*10.2*	*26.7*	*26.1*	*16.1*	*322.7*
Japanese yen	*21.7*	*18.9*	*23.1*	*30.0*	*18.3*	*11.8*	*15.3*	*24.7*	*159.4*
Swiss franc	*16.7*	*18.2*	*5.7*	*15.5*	*2.0*	*0.9*	*−3.9*	*3.5*	*119.8*
Deutsche mark	*12.9*	*21.2*	*9.4*	*7.3*	*1.5*	*14.0*	*6.2*	*1.3*	*110.7*
Ecu	*7.2*	*10.7*	*11.7*	*15.1*	*7.2*	*9.4*	*7.4*	*9.6*	*68.7*
Pound sterling	*9.2*	*11.7*	*11.3*	*9.5*	*8.2*	*10.4*	*10.2*	*7.6*	*62.8*
Other	*23.3*	*32.8*	*33.7*	*36.2*	*20.7*	*25.8*	*27.7*	*17.8*	*164.0*
Floating rate notes	12.1	23.5	27.1	42.1	1.0	5.1	10.5	27.1	205.7
US dollar	*3.9*	*7.0*	*10.2*	*15.0*	*−6.7*	*−9.2*	*−0.5*	*7.3*	*115.6*
Pound sterling	*2.2*	*10.5*	*8.9*	*10.5*	*2.2*	*9.0*	*7.0*	*6.4*	*42.7*
Other	*6.0*	*5.9*	*8.0*	*16.6*	*5.4*	*5.3*	*4.0*	*13.4*	*47.4*
Equity-related issues	43.4	42.0	85.2	33.2	38.0	34.1	74.8	23.2	258.7
US dollar	*29.2*	*29.0*	*65.1*	*19.6*	*25.8*	*26.2*	*60.4*	*16.0*	*169.2*
Swiss franc	*7.1*	*8.3*	*13.6*	*8.2*	*5.4*	*4.3*	*8.8*	*4.0*	*54.3*
Other	*7.0*	*4.7*	*6.5*	*5.4*	*6.8*	*3.6*	*5.5*	*3.1*	*35.2*

Exhibit 2.5.   Type and currency structure of international bond issues. *Sources:* **Bank of England, AIBD, and BIS.**

Page 2 · 13, replace Exhibit 2.6 with:

Type of Swap	1983	1984	1985	1986	1987	1988	1989	1990(a)
Currency	5	19	50	100	150	175	180	95
Interest Rate(b)	30	90	175	190	388	568	750	561
Total	35	109	225	290	538	743	930	656

(a) First half only

(b) Excluding other derivative instruments related to interest rate swaps, such as swaptions, caps, and floors, of which the notional principal value outstanding at the end of 1989 was $450 billion.

Exhibit 2.6. Estimated Notional Value of Swaps Arranged (in $ Billions) *Source:* **International Swap Dealers Association, BIS, Bank of England,** *The Economist.*

Page 2 · 13, replace Exhibit 2.7 with:

	1986 $	1987 $	1988 $	1989 $	1990 $	1991E $
Gross Equity Flows						
• Cross-Border	800.8	1,344.4	1,212.6	1,598.1	1,441.2	1,475.0
• Cross-Exchange	100.7	508.6	342.6	582.9	873.9	825.0
Total (A)	901.5	1,853.0	1,555.2	2,181.0	2,315.1	2,300.0
Equity Holdings (B)	460.0	520.4	625.0	830.0	683.0	840.0
Turnover Ratio (A/B)	1.96	3.56	2.49	2.63	3.39	2.75

Exhibit 2.7.   The size of the international equity market, 1986–91E (US$ in bns). *Source:* **Salomon Brothers.**

Page 2 · 15, replace Exhibit 2.9 with:

Year	Domestic U.S.		Cross Border						Outside U.S.		Global Totals	
			Buyer US		Seller US		Total X-border					
	#	$M	#	$M	#	$M	#	$M	#	$M	#	$M
1985	804 (868)	192,863.2	25 (57)	3,854.9	76 (109)	9,999.1	101 (163)	13,854.0	143 (106)	20,721.3	1048 (1,137)	227,438.5
1986	1178 (1,288)	203,985.7	39 (50)	2,918.4	164 (144)	31,126.8	203 (194)	34,045.2	296 (203)	38,728.9	1677 (1,685)	276,759.8
1987	1311 (1,311)	205,814.3	52 (89)	8,492.5	187 (135)	36,940.3	239 (224)	45,432.8	586 (366)	86,602.5	2136 (1,901)	337,849.6
1988	1580 (1,249)	294,429.7	81 (127)	6,687.6	247 (175)	61,450.9	328 (302)	68,138.5	1452 (858)	124,230.1	3360 (2,409)	486,798.3
1989	1872 (1,705)	244,793.3	149 (213)	25,336.3	405 (236)	52,393.2	554 (449)	77,729.5	1832 (1,575)	203,032.9	4258 (3,729)	525,555.7
1990	1564 (2,332)	106,802.1	143 (237)	20,896.8	398 (325)	50,458.2	541 (562)	71,355	1986 (1,565)	204,448.1	4091 (4,549)	382,605.2
1991	1139 (1,666)	48,032.8	133 (228)	8,268.5	212 (187)	8,152.8	345 (415)	16,421	1354 (1,299)	83,237.8	2838 (1,752)	147,691.9
Totals	9448 (10,419)	1,296,721.1	622 (1,001)	76,455.0	1689 (1,311)	250,521.3	2311 (2,309)	326,976.3	7649 (5,972)	761,001.6	19408 (17,162)	2,384,699.0

[a] Completed transactions include mergers, tender-mergers, tender offers, purchases of stakes, divestitures, recapitalizations, exchange offers, and LBOs.
[b] The volume data are classified according to the announcement date of a transaction—not taking into consideration when a transaction is completed.
[c] Million dollars of purchase price—excluding fees and expenses—at current exchange rates. The dollar value includes the amount paid for all common stock, common stock equivalents, preferred stock, debt, options, assets, warrants, and stake purchases made within six months of the announcement date of the transaction. Liabilities assumed are included if they are disclosed in press releases or newspaper articles.

Exhibit 2.9. Volume of completed international merger and corporate transactions[a,b]—United States (1985–1991) (in millions of U.S. dollars)[c]. Source: Securities Data Corporation, Mergers and Corporate Transactions database.

2.4 GLOBAL FINANCIAL MARKETS IN THE 1990s.

Page 2 · 17, replace Exhibit 2.10 with:

		New Issues				Stocks			
Issuers		1987	1988	1989	1990 in Billions	1985 of US Dollars	1988	1989	1990
Japan	A	42.4	50.8	96.7	57.9				
	B	36.5	40.3	83.8	38.5	64.1	183.6	265.3	317.7
United States	A	22.5	17.2	16.9	21.9				
	B	11.4	6.1	−0.3	1.5	102.7	165.5	162.5	170.3
United Kingdom	A	11.1	26.4	24.8	23.2				
	B	9.4	20.1	21.6	16.8	29.8	82.8	98.4	127.8
Canada	A	9.0	12.9	13.3	13.0				
	B	2.1	5.8	4.1	4.2	68.6	97.1	100.6	107.9
France	A	8.4	16.4	13.4	18.1				
	B	3.2	10.0	9.2	10.8	39.0	65.3	74.0	90.8
Other developed countries[1]	A	60.4	77.1	69.1	68.3				
	B	36.6	48.1	42.0	34.4	149.9	328.6	365.5	429.7
Developing countries[2]	A	2.0	3.8	2.5	7.0				
	B	−1.1	−1.0	−0.9	2.7	27.9	31.7	29.4	33.3
Eastern Europe	A	0.6	1.2	1.9	1.7				
	B	0.5	1.2	1.8	1.6	0.7	3.2	5.1	7.3
International institutions	A	19.5	20.5	23.1	30.6				
	B	8.4	7.6	12.9	20.5	89.9	140.4	151.5	187.7
Total	A	175.9	226.3	261.8	241.7				
	B	107.0	138.1	174.3	131.0	572.5	1,098.2	1,252.3	1,472.5

Note: A = announced gross new issues; B = completed new issues, net of repayments.
[1] Other BIS reporting countries plus non-reporting developed countries.
[2] OPEC and non-OPEC developing countries.

Exhibit 2.10.   Nationality of international bond issuers. *Sources:* Bank of England, AIBD, and BIS.

Page 2 · 22, replace Exhibit 2.13 with:

Year	All Companies (in percentages)	Manufacturing Sector (in percentages)
1975	62.8	69.0
1976	39.6	44.4
1977	41.5	42.3
1978	44.7	30.8
1979	36.7	23.9
1980	33.3	30.0
1981	35.5	28.6
1982	35.8	28.0
1983	35.9	24.5
1984	28.6	16.1
1985	27.0	13.3
1986	26.5	11.8
1987	18.9	4.4
1988	0.0	0.9
1989		(0.6)[a]
1990		(5.3)[a]

[a] Net financial *receipts,* that is, investment income, exceeded interest charges in manufacturing.

Exhibit 2.13.   Net financial costs (interest charges) as a percentage of operating profits, Tokyo Stock Exchange first-section companies, fiscal year 1975–88E. *Source:* **Tokyo Stock Exchange.**

CHAPTER 3

INTERNATIONALIZATION OF THE FINANCIAL SERVICES INDUSTRY

Ingo Walter
New York University and INSEAD

SUPPLEMENT CONTENTS

Page 3 • 5, add new section:

3.3A A FRAMEWORK FOR FINANCIAL INTERMEDIATION (NEW). An important prerequisite for understanding domestic and international financial intermediation, and hence the globalization of commercial and investment banking, is an appreciation for the nature of the conduits through which the financial assets of ultimate savers flow-through to the liabilities of the ultimate users of finance, both within and between regional and national economies. This involves alternative and competing modes of financial intermediation, or "contracting" between counterparties in financial transactions.

(a) Stylized Process of Financial Intermediation. A convenient "model" that can be used to guide thinking on financial contracting and the role of financial institutions and markets can be summarized in Figure 3.4A. The diagram depicts the financial process (flow-of-funds) among the different sectors of the economy in terms of the underlying environmental and regulatory determinants or drivers, discussed earlier, as well as the generic advantages needed to profit from the three primary intersectoral linkages:

- Savings/commercial banking and other traditional forms of intermediated finance.
- Investment banking and securitized intermediation.
- Various financial direct-connect mechanisms between borrowers and lenders.

Ultimate sources of surplus funds arise in the household sector (deferred consumption or savings), the corporate sector (retained earnings or business savings), and the government sector (budgetary surpluses).

Under the first or "classic" model of financial intermediation, savings (or funds sources) are held in the form of deposits or alternative types of liability claims issued by commercial banks, savings organizations, insurance companies or other forms of financial institutions entitled to finance themselves by placing their liabilities directly with the general public. Financial institutions then use these funds flows (liabilities) to purchase domestic and international assets issued by nonfinancial institution agents such as firms and governments.

Under the second model of funds flows, savings may be allocated directly to the purchase of securities publicly issued and sold by various government and private sector organizations in the domestic and international financial markets.

Under the third alternative, savings surpluses may be allocated directly to borrowers through various forms of private placement and other direct-sale mechanisms.

Ultimate users of funds comprise the same three segments of the economy: the household or consumer sector, the business sector, and the government sector.

Consumers may finance purchases by means of personal loans from banks or by loans secured by purchased assets (hire-purchase or installment loans). These may appear on the asset side of the balance sheets of credit institutions on a revolving basis for the duration of the respective loan contracts, or they may be sold off into the financial market in the form of securities backed by consumer credit receivables.

Corporations may borrow from banks in the form of unsecured or asset-backed straight or revolving credit facilities and/or may sell debt obligations (e.g., commercial paper, receivables financing, fixed-income securities of various types) or equities directly into the financial market.

Governments may likewise borrow from credit institutions (sovereign borrowing) or issue securities directly.

With the exception of consumers, other borrowers such as corporations and governments also have the possibility of privately issuing and placing their obligations with institutional investors, thereby circumventing both credit institutions and the public debt and equity markets. But even consumer debt can be repackaged as asset-backed securities and sold to private investors.

(b) Alternative Modes of Financial Contracting.   In the first mode of financial contracting, depositors buy the "secondary" financial claims or liabilities issued by credit institutions and benefit from liquidity, convenience, and safety through the ability of financial institutions to diversify risk and improve credit quality through professional asset management and monitoring of their holdings of primary financial claims (debt and equity). Savers can choose among a set of standardized contracts and receive payments services and interest that may or may not be subject to varying degrees of government regulation.

In the second mode, investors may select their own portfolios of financial assets directly from among the publicly issued debt and equity instruments on offer. This may provide a broader range of options than standardized bank contracts, and permit the large investors to tailor portfolios more closely to their objectives while still achieving acceptable liquidity through rapid execution of trades—aided by linkages with banks and other financial institutions that are part of the domestic payments mechanism. Small investors may choose to have their portfolios professionally managed, for a fee, through various types of mutual funds.

In the third mode, investors buy large blocks of privately issued securities. In doing so, they often face a liquidity penalty—due to the absence or limited availability of a liquid secondary market—for which they are rewarded by a higher yield. Recent institutional and regulatory developments have added to the liquidity of some direct-placement markets.

Value to ultimate savers and investors, inherent in the financial processes just described, accrues in the form of a combination of yield, safety, and liquidity. Value to ultimate users of funds accrues in the form of a combination of financing cost, transactions cost, flexibility, and liquidity. This value can be enhanced through credit backstops, guarantees, and derivative instruments such as forward rate agreements, caps, collars, futures, and options. Furthermore, markets can be linked functionally and geographically, both domestically and internationally.

Functional linkages permit bank receivables, for example, to be repackaged and sold to non-bank securities investors. Privately placed securities, once seasoned, may be able to be sold in public markets.

Geographic linkages make it possible for savers and issuers to gain incremental benefits in nonforeign and offshore markets, thereby enhancing liquidity and yield or reducing transaction costs.

If permitted by financial regulation, various kinds of financial firms emerge to perform the roles identified in Figure 3.4A—commercial banks, savings banks, postal savings institutions, savings cooperatives, credit unions, securities firms (full-service firms and various kinds of specialists), mutual funds, insurance companies, finance companies, finance subsidiaries of industrial companies, and various others. Members of each strategic group compete with each other, as well as with members of other strategic groups. Assuming it is allowed to do so, each organization elects to operate in one or more of the three financial-process modes identified in Exhibit 3.4A, according to its own competitive advantages, that is, its relative efficiency in the relevant financial production mode compared to that of other firms.

(c) Static and Dynamic Efficiency Aspects. Issues relating to the static and dynamic efficiency of the three alternative financial processes are depicted in Figure 3.4B.

Static efficiency is modeled as the all-in, weighted average spread (differential) between rates of return provided to ultimate savers and the cost of funds to users. This "gap," or spread, depicts the overall cost of using a particular mode or type of financial process. In particular, it reflects the direct costs of production (operating and administrative costs, cost of capital, etc.). It also reflects losses incurred in the financial process, as well as any monopoly profits earned and liquidity premia. Financial processes that are considered "statically inefficient" are usually characterized by high "spreads" due to high overhead costs, high losses, barriers to entry, and the like.

Dynamic efficiency is characterized by high rates of financial product and process innovation through time. Successful product and process innovation broadens the menu of financial products available to ultimate issuers, ultimate savers, or other agents along the various financial process channels just described. Probably the most powerful catalyst affecting the competitive dynamics of the financial services industry has been technological change, as discussed next.

It is against a background of continuous innovation that financial markets and institutions have evolved and converged (Smith & Walter, 1991). Global financial markets for foreign exchange, debt, and to a lesser extent equity have developed various degrees of "seamlessness." Indeed, it is arguable that the most advanced Western financial markets are approaching a theoretical, "complete" optimum where there are sufficient financial instruments and markets, and combinations thereof, to span the whole state-space of risk and return outcomes. Financial systems that are deemed inefficient or incomplete are characterized by a limited range of financial services and obsolescent financial processes.

Both static and dynamic efficiency are obviously important from the standpoint of national and global resource allocation, not only within the financial services industry itself but also as it effects users of financial services. That is, since financial services can be viewed as "inputs" to the overall real production process, along with labor and capital, the level of national output and income—as well as its rate of economic growth—are directly affected. A "retarded" financial services sector can represent a major impediment to a nation's overall real economic performance as is evident, for example, in the inability of the Eastern European countries to privatize companies expeditiously in the absence of a viable capital market.

In terms of Exhibit 3.4B, such retardation represents a burden on the final consumers of financial services and potentially reduce the level of private and social welfare. It also represents a burden on producers, by raising their cost structures and eroding their competitive performance in domestic and global markets. As such, they distort the patterns of allocation of

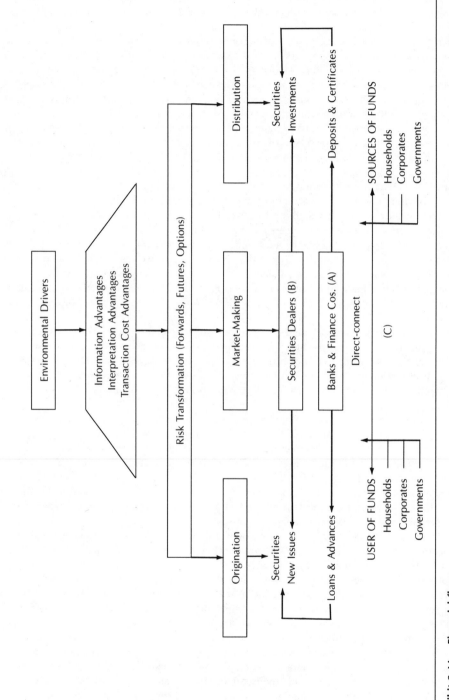

Exhibit 3.4A. Financial flows.

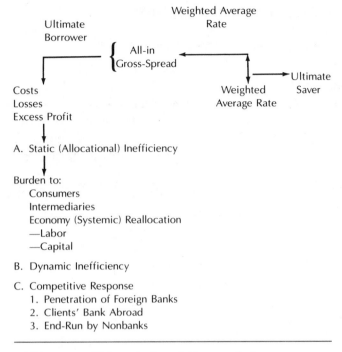

Exhibit 3.4B.   Efficiency in financial intermediation.

labor as well as capital. One major reason for progressive deregulation in many countries during the 1980s was an attempt to capture, for the countries involved, static and dynamic efficiency gains—and at the same time to capture the value-added generated in the financial services industry itself.

(d) Internationalizing the Model.   The stylized model of financial intermediation presented here is cast implicitly in the context of globally competing *domestic* financial systems. The process can itself, however, easily be globalized.

Sources of funds in national economies can be accessed by users of funds resident abroad. Examples include purchases of foreign securities by institutional investors and by domestic households, either as individual securities or through collective investment vehicles such as mutual funds. International access to national savings pools is of particular importance in view of the wide differences that exist in savings rates among countries.

Users of funds ranging from international organizations and government entities to corporations and even households (through asset-backed securities collateralized by consumer credit, mortgages, etc.) can access foreign sources of financing by borrowing or issuing securities outside the home country, either in foreign markets or in the offshore markets. International financings are particularly important in the light of large differences that exist in national levels of consumer, corporate, and governmental borrowing requirements.

Financial intermediaries connecting sources and users of funds operate internationally as well as domestically. Cross-border lending and foreign-currency funding are forms of international banking via the classic financial intermediation mode. Securities new issues incorporating international tranches link issuers and investors across national financial markets.

SOURCES AND SUGGESTED REFERENCES

Page 3 · 34, add the following reference after the sixteenth entry:

* Anthony Saunders and Ingo Walter, *Universal Banking in the United States* (New York: Oxford University Press, 1993).

Roy C. Smith and Ingo Walter, "Reconfiguration of Global Securities Markets in the 1990s," in Richard O'Brien (ed.) *Essays in Honor of Robert Marjolin: The 1990 Amex Bank Review Awards* (Cambridge: Cambridge University Press, 1991).

* Ingo Walter and Takato Hiraki (Eds.), *Restructuring Japan's Financial Markets* (Homewood, IL.: Business One/Irwin, 1993).

* Ingo Walter, *The Battle of the Systems* (Kiel: Institut for Weltwirtschaft, 1993).

CHAPTER 4

A SUMMARY OF ACCOUNTING PRINCIPLE DIFFERENCES AROUND THE WORLD

Philip R. Peller
Arthur Andersen & Co.

Frank J. Schwitter
Arthur Andersen & Co.

SUPPLEMENT CONTENTS

4.3 INTERNATIONAL ACCOUNTING DIVERSITY.

Page 4 · 3, replace Exhibit 4.1 with:

	United States	Japan	United Kingdom	France	Germany	Netherlands	Switzerland	Canada	Italy	Brazil
Capitalization of Research and Development Costs	Not Allowed	Allowed in certain circumstances	Allowed in certain circumstances	Allowed in certain circumstances	Allowed in certain circumstances	Allowed in certain circumstances	Allowed in certain circumstances	Allowed in certain circumstances	Allowed in certain circumstances	Allowed
Fixed Asset Revaluations Stated at Amount in Excess of Cost	Not Allowed	Not Allowed	Allowed	Allowed	Not Allowed	Allowed in certain circumstances	Allowed in certain circumstances	Not Allowed	Allowed in rare circumstances	Allowed
Inventory Valuation Using LIFO	Allowed	Allowed	Allowed but rarely done	Allowed	Allowed in certain circumstances	Allowed	Allowed	Allowed	Allowed	Allowed but rarely done
Finance Leases Capitalized	Required	Allowed in certain circumstances	Required	Allowed	Allowed in certain circumstances	Required	Allowed	Required	Not Allowed	Allowed but seldom done
Pension Expense Accrued During Period of Service	Required	Allowed	Required	Allowed	Required	Required	Allowed	Required	Allowed	Allowed
Book and Tax Timing Differences Presented on the Balance Sheet as Deferred Tax	Required	Allowed in certain circumstances	Required in certain circumstances	Required	Allowed but rarely done	Required	Allowed	Required	Allowed but rarely done	Required
Current Rate Method Used for Foreign Currency Translation	Required	Generally Required	Required	Generally required	Allowed	Required	Allowed	Required in certain circumstances	Required	Required
Pooling Method Used for Mergers	Required in certain circumstances	Allowed in certain circumstances	Allowed in certain circumstances	Not Allowed	Allowed in certain circumstances	Allowed but rarely done	Allowed but rarely done	Allowed in rare circumstances	Allowed in rare circumstances	Allowed but rarely done
Equity Method Used for 20–50% Ownership	Required	Required	Required	Required	Required	Required	Allowed	Required	Allowed	Required

Exhibit 4.1. Summary of principal accounting differences around the world.

4.5 ENVIRONMENTAL INFLUENCES ON ACCOUNTING.

Page 4 · 6, delete last sentence of third full paragraph.

4.6 FINANCIAL STATEMENT EFFECTS ON DIFFERENCES OF ACCOUNTING PRINCIPLES.

Page 4 · 7, delete reference to Germany in last sentence of last paragraph.

* *Page 4 · 8, delete reference to Brazil in first paragraph.*

* *Page 4 · 8, add sentence at end of first paragraph:*

In Brazil, Research and Development costs may be capitalized in all circumstances.

Page 4 · 9, delete last sentence of carryover paragraph.

Page 4 · 10, replace last complete sentence in last paragraph with:

As can be seen from Exhibit 4.1, all countries' standards listed here allow the LIFO method to be used under certain circumstances.

Page 4 · 11, delete first sentence of first full paragraph. Begin sentence with "In certain countries" as opposed to "In other countries."

Page 4 · 12, delete reference to France in last sentence of carryover paragraph.

Page 4 · 13, delete reference to Switzerland in last sentence of first full paragraph.

Page 4 · 13, delete reference to France in last sentence of last paragraph.

Page 4 · 17, replace last sentence of third paragraph with:

Canada requires the use of the temporal method for integrated foreign operations.

Page 4 · 18, delete last sentence of second full paragraph.

Page 4 · 19, delete reference to the United Kingdom in last sentence of fourth full paragraph.

CHAPTER 6

TAXONOMY OF AUDITING STANDARDS

Belverd E. Needles, Jr.
DePaul University

Thomas P. McDermott
Ernst & Young

Robert H. Tempkin
Ernst & Young

SUPPLEMENT CONTENTS

6.1 IMPORTANCE OF AUDITING STANDARDS AND THEIR HARMONIZATION.

Page 6 • 3, delete last three sentences of first full paragraph and the second full paragraph.

CHAPTER **6A**

*

MANAGING THE AUDIT RELATIONSHIP IN AN INTERNATIONAL CONTEXT (NEW)

Norman W. Walker
Price Waterhouse

CONTENTS

6A.1 INTRODUCTION. Professional accountants in their role as auditors perform an indispensable service in the financial reporting process. As independent outside experts, they audit management's financial representations and attest to their fairness. In doing so, they assure investors and other readers of published financial statements that the information they are using is relatively unbiased. This, in turn, contributes to the operational and allocational efficiency of the capital formation process.

Managing the audit relationship can be a challenging process for both the reporting entity as well as for the auditors seeking appointment. This is particularly true for international companies with worldwide operations as audit and accounting requirements vary from country to country (e.g., see the Appendix to this chapter as well as Chapters 6 and 14 of the *Handbook*).

Selecting auditors involves:

- Clearly identifying expectations of the auditors
- Assessing the qualifications of the candidates
- Establishing the deliverables or terms of reference.

Maintaining a successful relationship with auditors further involves evaluating performance, both the company's and the auditor's, and providing feedback in both directions.

Throughout the process of selecting and maintaining a relationship with auditors, communications are the most critical success factor. The challenges to successful communications for international companies and their auditors are many—language differences, time and distance differences, different and changing accounting and reporting requirements from country to country, and, most importantly, the differences in national cultures. After reading this chapter the reader should be better able to manage the selection and continuing relationship with auditors.

6A.2 ESTABLISHING EXPECTATIONS.   It is particularly important that a company focus on their expectations of their auditors if they wish to obtain the maximum value from the relationship. This should include clearly identifying those expectations and communicating them to the auditors.

(a) Scope of Services.   There are several dimensions to the question of what services the auditors are to provide. The annual audit of the group financial statements is the obvious starting point which, together with other aspects of the scope of possible services, is discussed next.

(i) The Audit.

SINGLE OR MULTIPLE AUDITORS.   Predominant practice is to appoint a single audit firm to perform an audit sufficient in scope to issue an opinion on the group financial statements. With operations in many locations and countries and possibly in different businesses, the audit of an international company's group financial statements requires communication and a high degree of coordination between the auditors involved as well as a clear understanding of their respective responsibilities. These auditors also require leadership, organization, and control by those who are responsible for the audit at the group or parent company level.

There are distinct advantages to appointment of a single audit firm as auditors to all subsidiaries in a group:

- The engagement partner at the group level is responsible for coordinating all service to the company. The company can look to one person to initiate action to meet their needs throughout the world.
- Comprehensive and timely reporting to the parent company's management, board of directors, and audit committee is greatly facilitated. Such matters as scope of work, audit findings, proposed audit reports, internal control, and other recommendations and fees can be reported promptly and efficiently for all locations.
- All of the offices of the audit firm throughout the world *should* subscribe to a common service philosophy and audit approach. If they do, they can work more effectively with each other in identifying and meeting the company's needs and resolving questions on auditing and accounting, format and content of reports, deadlines and billing arrangements. This compatibility contributes to audit efficiency because:

  —All offices act in harmony providing the most effective service to the group.
  —Information flows freely between offices, individual partners, and staff without unnecessary formality.

—Full advantage can be taken of opportunities to restrict audit scope at selected locations and to work with internal auditors. Also, audit scope can be communicated to other offices with less difficulty and less chance of misunderstanding.

—The principal office can more effectively monitor and control group audit fees by prompt receipt of details on estimated actual time and expenses.

—The company can choose to negotiate fees with the auditors on a worldwide basis or an individual location basis. If multiple auditors are involved, fee negotiations necessarily are required with each audit firm.

If more than one audit firm is used, there is also a question of divided responsibility for the opinion of the group financial statements. In circumstances where multiple audit firms are selected, as a minimum, the principal auditor generally must audit a majority of the group to issue a report on the group financial statements. What constitutes a majority of the group is determined by reference to the most appropriate criteria in the circumstances. Group consolidated assets and revenues are normally appropriate; however, net assets and earnings may also be important.

In some countries, the principal auditors are required to assume sole responsibility for the group audit report, even though other auditors examined part of the group. In other countries, the principal auditor has the option of indicating the division of responsibility by reference to the other auditors in his report. The predominant practice is for the principal auditors to refer to the other auditors if those auditors audit operations that are material to the group financial statements. In either case, the other auditors remain responsible for the performance of their work and for their own reports. A key consideration here is whether management and the board of directors wish to have sole responsibility for the audit of the group financial statements vested in a single firm of auditors.

While it is not particularly common, companies sometimes select audit firms to perform an audit jointly. In these circumstances, a single audit report may be issued over the signature of both firms or separate reports may be issued on the same set of financial statements. Any company expectations in this regard must be clearly set forth to the audit firm candidates at the outset, because firms may choose to accept such an engagement only in exceptional circumstances.

STATUTORY AUDIT REQUIREMENTS OUTSIDE THE PARENT COMPANY'S COUNTRY.   Many countries impose statutory audit requirements on subsidiaries or other business units located in that country. Frequently, these requirements extend only to companies that meet certain size requirements, normally total assets, annual revenue, or turnover and, occasionally, number of employees. The most common practice is to have most or all statutory audit requirements fulfilled by the audit firm responsible for auditing the group consolidated financial statements (i.e., the principal auditors).

However, this is not a requirement, even in circumstances where management and the board of directors of the company desire to have responsibility for the audit of the group financial statements vested in a single firm of auditors. Depending on the significance of individual operations to the group financial statements, the principal auditor may require audit procedures to be performed for those operations only occasionally or not at all. In effect, the audit scope is established in the context of the group financial statements. In such circumstances, the statutory audit requirements for those operations may be fulfilled either by the principal auditors or other auditors.

REVIEWS OF INTERIM FINANCIAL INFORMATION.   If reviews of quarterly or semi-annual financial information are required or desired by the company, there are several questions that must be addressed:

• Are the reviews to be performed on a "timely" basis, that is, contemporaneously with and immediately following the preparation of the interim financial information, or on a basis to coincide with completion of the annual audit?

• Are separate reports to be issued?

• If separate reports are to be issued, will they be available to shareholders or otherwise publicly?

The extent and timing of work to be performed by the auditors will vary depending on the answers to these questions. Further, the extent of reporting to the company on the results of the reviews may vary from the standard written reports prescribed by professional standards to oral or informal reporting to management or the board of directors on the results of the review and related observations that the auditors have for the company.

OTHER REPORTING REQUIREMENTS.   Frequently, there are statutory or other reporting requirements for the parent company or individual subsidiaries beyond those involved in the audit of the group financial statements. Such requirements may result from contractual requirements (e.g., lease or other debt agreements) or statutes of individual countries. The latter area includes audits of employee benefit plans for which reporting standards have been increasing significantly in recent years, thus requiring greater efforts on the part of both companies and their auditors. In addition, countries other than the United States are now requiring audits of such plans.

Further, reporting on compliance with legal regulations, company bylaws, proper handling of correspondence and minutes of meetings, and so on, may be required as in Colombia or a tax compliance "audit" may be required as in Mexico. In these cases, materiality standards may not apply and the penalties, and hence the risk, faced by the auditor in the event of an error in the reports or underlying information may be significant. Accordingly, the company's expectations of its auditors in these areas must be clearly understood by them.

RELIANCE ON INTERNAL AUDIT.   Internal audit capabilities at international companies range from very little to very extensive. Similarly, the focus of internal audit functions can range from project or program audits to systems and controls audits to full financial statement audits. Some companies desire that their external auditors place the maximum reliance possible, within the requirements of applicable professional standards, on their internal audit group. In other cases, international companies want their external auditors to place little or no reliance on their internal auditors. The effect on the scope of the external auditor's work from placing reliance on the internal auditors can be very significant, resulting in a similarly significant effect on external audit fees.

The degree to which external auditors are able to rely on the work of internal auditors is based on several factors, including:

• The degree of independence of the internal auditors within the company
• Their competence and experience
• The relevance of their work to the external auditors
• The adequacy of their working papers and reports
• How responses to their reports are monitored and implemented.

When the evaluation of each of these factors is very positive, the key issue becomes a question of allocation, within the confines of applicable professional standards, of the total audit effort between external and internal auditors.

TIMING.   Expectations as to timing of auditors' work and reporting are crucial to a company's successful relationship with those auditors. Audit firms are normally flexible and able to meet company desired timing for work and reporting. However, the concentration of December 31 year ends among companies, particularly in the United States, results in a peak load or "busy season" in the months of January through March. Most audit firms desire to move as much work as possible out of the busy season. In any event, the company's expectation for timing of the audit and related reporting must be clearly set forth. This includes:

- Opinion and earnings release dates
- Publishing dates for printed annual reports and reports filed with governmental agencies
- Audit committee and annual meeting dates.

(ii) Business Advice.   Historically, auditors have provided general business advice to companies they were serving on a variety of matters, including the effectiveness of the company's operations and organization, financial structure, policies, and regulatory matters. More recently, some companies have received only reports on the audit and reports on internal control or other matters as required by professional standards. This latter approach is sometimes referred to as a "commodity" purchase approach.

However, the challenges facing companies today, particularly international companies, are tremendous. Business environments are changing, in many cases rapidly, all around the world.

Auditors perform business risk assessments, obtain evidence as to the design and operation of control systems, and evidence with respect to specific transactions for all significant company operations worldwide. Further, auditors normally bring extensive experience with other companies, both in the same businesses and in other businesses to their task.

This combination of activities involved in performing an audit of the group financial statements, together with their extensive expertise from around the world, positions auditors to be a valued business advisor to international companies.

While it is less common for companies to focus on and articulate their expectations in the area of business advice than in the area of the specific audit requirements discussed above, it is no less critical to a successful and valued relationship between the company and their auditors.

Typical areas where business advice might be sought include:

- Cash management and treasury matters
- Management reporting and monitoring
- Stock options and other forms of incentive compensation
- Inventory management, including purchasing policies and procedures
- Business combinations (acquisitions)

The distinction between business advice that can be expected as a normal outgrowth of the audit process and tax or consulting projects that are discussed below is normally the amount of incremental time required on the part of the audit firm. Advice or recommendations to *consider* various courses of action generally flow from knowledge gained through the audit and prior experiences. Recommendations to *implement* specific courses of action or changes usually require a specific additional commitment of the audit firm's resources and would be considered a separate consulting project.

(iii) Performance Evaluation.   During the course of performing an audit, the auditors will work closely with finance, accounting, and internal audit personnel at all significant operations. The extent to which management wishes to receive an evaluation from the auditor regarding the personnel they have worked with varies from company to company. In some cases, management wishes only to be informed of extreme negative performance, that is, a negative exception basis. In other cases, management wants more thorough reporting of both positive and negative performance. Further, expectations may differ from operation to operation within a single company. In all cases, evaluating and reporting on performance of individuals is a delicate undertaking and must be performed with great care. Again, the company's expectations in this area must be clearly addressed.

(iv) Taxes.   As part of the audit of the group financial statements, the auditors are required to determine whether or not the impact of taxes, both income and other taxes, has been presented fairly in those financial statements. Beyond this requirement, and depending upon the company's

internal expertise in the area of taxes as well as other factors, the company may wish to involve the auditors in a variety of other tax planning and tax compliance activities of the company. These activities may vary from country to country and may also cover employees' personal taxes, particularly in the case of employees on international assignments.

While many companies receive significant tax services from their auditors, that is not always the case. If the engagement of auditors is to include such tax services on a recurring basis, the company's expectations should be clearly delineated.

(v) Consulting Projects.   Auditors gain substantial knowledge of the company's operations and its needs as a result of performing the audit. Most audit firms have significant expertise in selected areas outside of accounting and auditing and taxes. The knowledge gained through the performance of the audit can be leveraged with the other areas of expertise to provide information technology, due diligence, treasury operations, employee benefits, and other consulting services.

It is possible that providing consulting services to a company could be undertaken in such a manner that they become more decision making than advising or become so significant in amount that providing such services could compromise the auditor's independence. Regulations in some countries, such as the United States, specifically prohibit some activities (e.g., executive search) and place very restrictive limits on others. For example, bookkeeping services can only be provided in certain circumstances and, in any event, may not exceed 1% of worldwide audit fees.

It is prudent in all cases, and required in the case of public companies in the United States, that boards of directors or their audit committees actively monitor the consulting services provided by the company's auditors and conclude that such services have not in fact compromised the independence of the auditors.

(b) Communications.   As indicated in the introduction to this chapter, communications are the most critical success factor for international companies in selecting and maintaining a relationship with their auditors. The sections which follow discuss four aspects of communications, namely participants in the communications process and content, form, and frequency.

(i) Participants in the Communications Process.   Communications between an international company and their auditors is a "many to many" process. From the company's perspective, the board of directors, audit committee, chief executive officers, and/or managing directors, financial management, including finance and accounting officers, tax directors and treasury officers, internal auditors, chief information officers, and legal counsel are all important in the communications process. Communications are with individuals in the above positions or with those responsibilities at both the parent company and subsidiary or significant operating unit level.

From the auditor's perspective, the key individual in the communications process is normally the overall engagement partner at the parent company level. However, the tax and other partners who may be serving the company at the parent company level as well as the partners serving subsidiary companies or major operating units are also important to the process. In fact, a major challenge faced by the overall engagement partner on a day-to-day basis is to keep abreast of important communications between the auditors and the company on a worldwide basis.

Effective communications between auditors in various locations serving an international company involve a balancing act in meeting the apparently divergent needs of a multinational holding company and its subsidiaries. This balancing act may involve either professional issues or client relations matters. International companies must make their expectations in this regard very clear. The ultimate responsibility of the auditor normally must be to the parent or holding company. The needs of the parent company and the auditors' responsibilities to the parent company must be paramount.

(ii) Content.   The content or nature of communications between international companies and their auditors vary from statutorily required opinions and formal recommendations on matters of

internal control to a variety of matters that assist in maintaining an effective working relationship. This latter area includes:

- Engagement letters
- Plans for the audit
- New financial reporting and accounting matters
- Business advice, including changes in taxation and governmental regulation as well as opportunities for using new developments in information technology.
- Personnel evaluations
- Progress reports and significant matters noted during the conduct of the audit.

It is fundamental to an audit that the auditors have access to all relevant information underlying the company's financial statements. Beyond this, it is very important that the company communicate their expectations in all areas discussed in this section clearly and succinctly to their auditors if they expect their expectations to be fully satisfied.

(iii) Form.   At the heart of communications between a company and its auditors are written reports or presentations. The value of written communications in avoiding miscommunications cannot be overestimated. Even in meetings that feature oral presentations and discussion, written communications often form the underlying basis for the meeting.

The combination of significant distances and differences in time zones have long been recognized as a challenge to effective communications in international companies and among the auditors serving those companies. To overcome this hurdle, financial management from the parent company together with the engagement partner and managers for the parent company have visited major subsidiaries and lead meetings with the subsidiaries' financial and operating management and engagement partners and managers serving the subsidiary. This form of communication can be characterized by viewing the parent company financial management and engagement partners/managers as the hub of a wheel and the visits to the subsidiaries as spokes on the wheel.

More recently, many international companies and their auditors have conducted meetings on a worldwide or regional basis that bring both financial management and auditors from all subsidiaries together with the financial management and auditors from the parent company level. While such meetings entail the commitment of time and economic resources, the advantages to be gained are numerous.

From the company's perspective, the opportunity to

- Describe their business vision and discuss their specific needs
- Address the priority issues, opportunities and threats to be faced both in the short-term and in the long-term
- Discuss the related actions planned or underway
- Outline the methods used to measure success
- Relate what is expected from their auditors.

From the auditor's perspective, the opportunity to

- Gain insights into the company's needs
- Secure feedback on the company's expectations
- Improve communications with the company's decision makers
- Promote the exchange of ideas and experiences
- Subdue time and space barriers.

These meetings can be viewed as the rim on the wheel discussed in the preceding paragraph. Personal acquaintance can go a long way to removing the barriers to effective communication.

(iv) Frequency.   As with the nature of communications, the frequency of some communications between a company and its auditors is required by professional standards or statutory regulation and the frequency of such communications (e.g., audit committee meetings) follows naturally from the audit process. With respect to other communications, the expectation is normally to avoid surprises. This means early communication of any matters that could present a significant problem for the company or jeopardize the timeliness or success of completion of the services being provided. The watchword for both the company and auditors should be "when in doubt, communicate." While the volume of communications encountered through the in-basket (either paper or electronic) and phone mail can be daunting, that will never be a satisfactory explanation in hindsight for the failure to communicate an important matter on a timely basis.

(c) Consistency of Service.   With few exceptions, companies seek a consistently high level of service from their auditors, both over time and at all locations around the world where the companies are being served. However, it is useful to recognize the factors that can impact achieving a consistent high level of service.

First and foremost is a commitment on the part of both the company and the auditors to a consistent high level of service. The most able audit organization in the world will have difficulty overcoming a severe lack of cooperation from an international company. Responsiveness to the needs of the auditors, whether they be for access to key individuals, information, or answers to questions raised is crucial to the auditor's success in consistently delivering high quality services.

Another factor that must be considered in establishing an expectation for a consistent level of service worldwide is the availability of top quality people in some parts of the world. For a variety of reasons, international companies may have significant operations in areas of the world where the supply of well-trained financial personnel is extremely limited. This can impact both the company and the auditors in those locations. Traditionally, both parties have sought to address this situation by sending individuals from areas where there is an ample supply of financial expertise to those locations where there isn't. While this may meet the immediate need, the approach is also not without its drawbacks. Specifically, it is difficult to assimilate the national culture and business environment in these locations quickly. It may not be possible for the expatriots to gain acceptance into the business community with the insights and understandings that such acceptance brings, except over a fairly long period of time.

Both with respect to consistency over time and consistency from location to location, a critical element is feedback from the company to the auditors on their performance. Simply put, the auditors need to know, for better or for worse, how they're doing. The company should commit to providing feedback on a periodic basis that is consistent in coverage with the scope of services being provided by the auditors. While the specific performance measures to be included in the feedback may vary from company to company, they typically would include subjects such as:

- Sensitivity to the company's needs
- Business perspective
- Technical knowledge and expertise
- Proactivity
- Coordination of services
- Engagement team characteristics
- Fees and cost control
- Communication.

As already mentioned, the last performance measure, communications, is probably the most important.

6A.3 ASSESSING THE QUALIFICATIONS OF THE CANDIDATES.   There are numerous criteria that can be used to assess the qualifications of the firms being considered for selection as auditors. Some of the criteria may be assessed fairly objectively and it is likely that different companies assessing the same firm of auditors would make a similar assessment. In other cases, the assessments are very subjective and different companies might make very different assessments of the same firm. A company's assessment of a particular firm may differ substantially based on the engagement team proposed by that firm.

It is almost always useful to adopt a relatively straight forward quantitative framework for assessing a firm's qualifications. Such a framework might entail rating each of the criteria for each of the firms on a scale of, say, 1 to 5 or 1 to 10. A further step would be to group the criteria into those that are most important, of moderate importance, or of lesser importance; and assign a rating of 1, 2, or 3 to the criteria within those groups, respectively. As useful as the quantitative framework may be in focusing the assessment of the firms, it must be recognized that the final decision may come down to a subjective choice between the top competitors. That choice may not be the firm with the best quantitative score.

(a) Criteria.   The criteria discussed in the following paragraphs form the basis for the selection of auditors by international companies. The criteria are not necessarily presented in the order of their importance, as that is a relative judgment and, in all likelihood, will differ from company to company. However, in virtually every case, each of these criteria should be taken into consideration as well as others that individual companies may identify.

(i) Experience in Serving International Companies.   Experience in serving similarly configured international companies is invaluable to auditors in providing high quality service to a new international company client. This is important both for the offices serving the parent company as well as for offices serving subsidiaries or other major operating units, or in the vernacular of audit firms, both the office sending instructions and the office receiving instructions.

Further, the partners and managers assigned to the engagement teams at both the parent company level and the subsidiary level should have verifiable experience serving international companies. While it may not be the most important factor, it is, nonetheless, very desirable for the engagement team to have experience both as a team sending instructions as well as a team receiving instructions. Such experience clearly benefits effective communications and the anticipation of potential problems in carrying out their respective assignments.

Relevant direct international experience is a definite plus for all partners and managers serving an international company. Such experience includes tours of duty in locations outside of one's home country as well as specific client assignments of more than brief duration outside one's home country. Such tours and assignments should benefit the engagement team members and, hence, the company immeasurably in understanding the business environments in different countries and in becoming aware of the impact the national cultures have on how business is conducted.

Foreign language proficiency is desirable. In fact, since international companies often operate in many countries, numerous languages are encountered and multiple foreign capability would be very beneficial. Unfortunately, individuals' foreign language capabilities are often limited to a single additional language at the day-to-day working level. The prevalence of English as a common language in business mitigates some of the potential language problem. In some situations (e.g., Japanese and Chinese), the use of interpreters is fairly common. If the interpreters have worked with auditors frequently they can compensate for what otherwise would be, literally, "lost in translation."

(ii) Coverage of Company Locations.   An audit firm's ability to deliver quality service is directly related to whether they have full time partners and staff in close proximity to an international company's subsidiaries or other significant operating units. The option of flying professional staff in to provide recurring services is rarely successful. Obtaining and maintaining

a deep understanding of the company's business operations and being fully responsive to the company's needs are quite difficult on a fly-in basis. Such arrangements should be avoided wherever possible.

(iii) Knowledge of the Company's Industries.   Knowledge of the company's industries rarely rates below the highest level when considering criteria for the selection of auditors. Such knowledge is vital to assessing risk in the audit process and understanding management's perspective in addressing issues and challenges they face.

If the auditors understand the critical success factors in the company's industries as well as the company's specific operations, they are better able to assist audit risk with respect to the company's reported financial position, results of operations and cash flows. Further, this knowledge contributes directly to the auditor's ability to provide valued business advice, as discussed above.

It is not reasonable to expect the same depth and breadth of industry and business knowledge at every company location around the world. However, the auditors should have or be willing to relocate such experience to directly serve the parent company. In addition, it is important to identify backup capability within the auditor's organization in the event that the company should need to draw on that capability for whatever reason.

(iv) Communications Capabilities.   As stressed throughout this chapter, communications are the most important link for international companies in having a successful relationship with their auditors. Facsimile and phone mail communications tools have become commonplace for virtually all organizations. They have contributed to vastly improved communications as compared to 10 years ago. More recently, electronic mail between companies and their auditors at all locations have provided a new boost to timely communication. The ability to send electronic documents, analyses, and files between the company and their auditors and between the auditors serving the parent company and those serving the subsidiaries and vice versa should be expected. The ability to communicate in this fashion enhances both the timeliness of communication as well as the efficiency of the audit process.

While video conferencing has not been used extensively to date in communications between companies and their auditors at various locations around the world, the audit organizations views and expectations on that communications form should be assessed. In light of the expense and time involved in extensive global travel and in view of the effectiveness of video conferencing, particularly for people who have worked together on a face-to-face basis in the past, video conferencing capability should be carefully considered by international companies in working with their auditors in the future.

(v) Working with Internal Auditors.   For international companies who have the expectation that their external auditors will rely on the work of internal auditors to more than an insignificant extent, it is important to assess the external audit firm's approach to relying on internal audit and their track record in that regard. This assessment should be specific to the particular engagement team proposed at the parent company level. Further, if the company has internal audit activity both in the parent country and in other countries around the world, the external auditor's record should be evaluated with respect to working with internal audit in a comparable manner.

Companies may also wish to consider whether the external auditors are familiar with the professional standards promulgated by internal audit professional organizations and whether the external auditor could evaluate and assist in improving the quality of internal audit practice in the company.

(vi) Continuity.   Knowledge of the company, its industries and businesses on the part of the service providers is a key ingredient. Rarely can such knowledge be gained in the course of a single year's audit engagement. In fact, at least 2 or 3 years' experience is normally necessary for the partners serving a company to be in a position to provide the greatest value to the company.

Professional standards in some countries limit the period of time that professionals can serve a specific company, generally 5 to 7 years for partners and lesser periods for managers or other professional staff. Within these limitations, it generally behooves a company to keep the engagement partners for as long as possible and to obtain a "fresh look" periodically through the rotation of other professionals assigned to the engagement team.

Again, companies should seek verification of an audit firm's track record in providing continuous service at the partner and manager level from existing clients, particularly international companies in similar situations.

(vii) Responsiveness and Quality of Advice and Recommendations.   Over time, the evaluation of the success of a relationship with an audit firm will often come down to judgment about the responsiveness and quality of the advice and recommendations received from the auditors. There are several factors which are considered in making those judgments:

- Early identification of issues or opportunities and communication of those matters to appropriate members of the company's management
- Timely and appropriate responses to specific needs
    —if the need is urgent, the response reflects the urgency
    —bringing the right resources within the audit firm to bear and getting the benefit of that firm's whole knowledge base
- Quality of both written and oral reports and recommendations
    —demonstrate an in-depth knowledge of the specific circumstances and the overall business
    —concise and understandable
    —sensitive to company's culture and style
    —represent sound business advice.

Assessing such factors during the initial selection process requires reviewing actual reports issued (names deleted where appropriate) by the audit firms and discussions with clients of the firms. These discussions should include both existing and former clients, as the latter may have some very enlightening and sometimes surprising perspectives on the responsiveness and quality criteria.

(viii) Plans for Serving the Company.   The starting point for providing professional services to an international company is the preparation of an overall or strategic plan for those services. Such a plan is imperative for effectively and efficiently serving a worldwide company. Each final candidate in the selection process should compare and present their strategic plan to the company.

There are several aspects of such plans that the company's evaluation should be directed to:

- Does the plan reflect and respond to the expectations of the company as discussed earlier in this chapter?
- Does the plan demonstrate an understanding of the company's operations, including business strategies and operating plans?
- Does the plan reflect reasonable assessments of the relative levels of business and audit risk associated with various company operations?
- Are financial reporting and accounting areas involving a significant degree of subjectivity identified?
- Does the plan reflect a sound assessment of the company's control environment and information systems environments?
- Does the plan include a commitment of professional resources commensurate with the services to be provided?

- Are the preliminary decisions about the overall audit approach at the parent company and significant subsidiaries or other operating units consistent with the assessments of business and audit risk, control environment and information systems environment? Are those decisions responsible to specific company expectations?

The depth of knowledge obtained by auditors during a proposal process will be substantially less than after having provided significant services to the company. Nevertheless, the strategic plan presented during the proposal should demonstrate persuasively to the company that the audit firm is proceeding on a sound basis. Further, it should confirm the company's assessment of the responsiveness and quality of the audit firm's oral and written reports or presentations referred to above.

(ix) Chemistry. The most subjective criteria involved in the assessment process is determining how well the proposed engagement team fits with the international company's culture and style. It must be recognized that over time members of both the engagement team and company management will change and a fit for today may not be a fit for tomorrow.

To properly assess this criteria requires that quality time be spent with the proposed engagement team members during the assessment process. While part of this time may be represented by formal meetings and discussion, often informal contacts provide a very good basis for making the assessment. Traveling with engagement team members to visit subsidiaries or significant company operations around the world is frequently a good way to foster such informal contacts.

Engagement team members should demonstrate a healthy respect for the company's culture and style. This aspect encompasses interpersonal relations, conversational language, punctuality, dress, social contacts, format for meetings, enthusiasm, and energy level, and so on. Again, in the initial selection of auditors, the most useful source of such information is from current and former clients. Particularly with respect to this criteria, the evaluation should be specific to the proposed engagement team members.

Many international companies have a large number of partners and managers from the audit firm providing service on a worldwide basis. It is useful to have the managing director and financial management at significant subsidiaries also assess the chemistry of their local engagement team partners and managers. However, the key focus should be on the parent company engagement team partners and managers because the involvement with them will be the most extensive and they will set the tone for the worldwide engagement teams. In fact, the parent company engagement partner should have considerable influence over the initial selection and any subsequent changes in the partners serving the company on a worldwide basis. The parent company engagement partner has overall responsibility for the performance of the worldwide team.

(x) Cost. The competitiveness of the marketplace for professional services provided by audit firms is well known to all participants, worldwide. The fees paid to audit firms by an international company will, first and foremost, reflect the expectations discussed in the previous section of this chapter and will vary considerably from international company to international company. Within that context, audit firms are very competitive, both at the time of initial selection as well as on a continuing basis. This latter point reflects the fact that, while audit firms realize it is costly, particularly in terms of time, for international companies to change audit firms, such changes have and will continue to take place if the value received by the international companies is not commensurate with the fees being charged.

Whatever the level of the international company's expectations with respect to its auditors, the efficiency with which the services are delivered will be strongly influenced by the coordination and cooperation between the company and the auditors. Such coordination and cooperation is important not just with respect to the internal auditing activity, but with respect to operating as well as financial and accounting personnel. The lack of availability of key operating personnel can provide the necessary understanding of the company operation and explanations for the financial impacts of those operations can significantly affect the efficiency of the audit process.

Historically, fees for audit services were generally negotiated and agreed upon by financial management and the engagement partners at the individual operating unit level. Such an approach has the advantage from the company's perspective of being able to match closely the value of services received with the fees paid for those services. However, across large international companies, apparent anomalies in fee levels could result between operating units that would appear to require similar levels of service.

More recently, many international companies have negotiated and agreed upon a single worldwide fee. Negotiations normally are between the financial management at the corporate or parent company level and the audit firms engagement partner at the comparable level. The global fee is then allocated by the audit firm to the various offices serving the international company. The global approach has the obvious benefit of overall cost control but also entails the risk of not fairly reflecting circumstances and differences in individual operating units.

An example of the latter can occur in highly inflationary countries. In those countries, rates of inflation do not necessarily correspond to the devaluation of the local currency versus hard currencies at the official exchange rates. Typically, companies have tended to fix the audit fees in those countries in a hard currency. If the devaluation does not properly match the inflation, the impact of the audit firm in that country can be severe and unwarranted. In such circumstances, it is desirable, if not imperative, to allow local adjustment of the fee after the services have been provided and inflation/devaluation factors known to maintain a productive working relationship between the auditors and the company.

In the final analysis, there are two questions that international companies must answer in judging the fees paid to auditors:

- Is the value received commensurate with the fee being paid?
- Are the fees reasonably competitive?

If the answer to the first question is no, the second question is not relevant. If the answer to the first question is yes but the answer to the second question is no, the international company will undoubtedly seek an adjustment from their auditors. In all but very rare cases, an appropriate adjustment will be agreed.

6A.4 ESTABLISHING THE TERMS OF REFERENCE OR DELIVERABLES.   The final step in the process is to formalize the terms of reference or deliverables in an engagement letter or memoranda of services to be provided by the audit firm selected.

(a) Rationale.   While engagements have been undertaken by auditors on the basis of an oral or handshake agreement only, the extent and complexity of providing professional services to an international company requires more formal arrangements. The process of establishing expectations and assessing the qualifications of the firms normally involves considerable discussions over several weeks' time. The number of individuals involved in receiving services in an international company as well as the number of partners responsible for the delivery of services for the audit firm can be very large. Further, the individuals involved on both sides will, over time, change. In such circumstances, it is necessary to clarify through a written document the understandings that have been reached and thereby avoid misunderstandings of the intended arrangements at a later date.

(b) Content.   All significant objective aspects of the company's expectations discussed in the first section of this chapter should be included in the terms of reference. Such items would include:

- All audit and related reports to be received
- Reliance on an anticipated and coordination with internal audit
- Tax and consulting projects, if applicable
- Timing of work and related reporting.

The commitment of company resources for clerical and administrative support should also be clearly spelled out. Such assistance can be critical in meeting reporting deadlines and providing service in the most efficient manner possible.

Fee arrangements including the timing and amounts of billings, to whom bills should be submitted, any special approval requirements and payment terms should be included. While such matters may seem mundane, they can be a disruption to an otherwise strong working relationship between an international company and its auditors.

A final matter to consider for inclusion in the terms of reference is the company's plan for reviewing the performance of the audit firm. A brief description of the timing and focal points of the performance review will be useful to both parties. With respect to timing, a review should be performed after the first year. Taking the time to provide such feedback will be very beneficial to the audit firm and allow them to make what will inevitability be necessary corrections in their approach to serving the company. After the initial year, reviews every two or three years would be optimal.

6A.5 CONCLUSION.   Changing audit firms is time consuming and inherently inefficient with respect to at least the first (if not the second and third) annual audit after the change. International companies have more at risk in this regard because of the worldwide nature and extent of their needs.

As stated in this chapter, the keys to maintaining a successful relationship between an international company and its auditors, and thus avoiding a change, are:

- Clearly identified expectations
- Careful assessment of qualifications
- Thorough evaluation of performance
- Communications, communications, communications!

Valued, mutually beneficial relationships have been maintained by international companies and their auditors for decades. Adherence to the matters noted above are at the heart of those successful relationships.

APPENDIX A: SUMMARY OF NATIONAL AUDIT REQUIREMENTS.

Argentina	Finland	Korea
Australia	France	Mexico
Austria	Gabon	Morocco
Barbados	Germany	Namibia
Belgium	Greece	The Netherlands
Brazil	Hong Kong	New Zealand
Canada	India	Nicaragua
Cayman Islands	Ireland, Northern	Norway
Chile	Ireland, Republic of	Papua New Guinea
Colombia	Italy	Peru
Denmark	Jamaica	Philippines
El Salvador	Japan	Portugal

Puerto Rico	Switzerland	United Kingdom
Saudi Arabia	Taiwan	United States
Singapore	Tanzania	Uruguay
South Africa	Thailand	Venezuela
Spain	Trinidad & Tobago	Zaire
Sweden	Turkey	Zimbabwe

Argentina.

An annual GAAS audit is required by law and there are no criteria for exemption.

Local audits do not significantly differ from IFAC guidelines.

Australia.

An annual GAAS audit is required by law, however, no audit is required if the company is an "exempt propriety company." These are private companies where there is no ownership or interest either directly or indirectly held by a public company and there is unanimous consent by members. They are still required to produce unaudited financial statements. Also, no audit is required if a company is 100% owned by another Australian company and the company has entered into a mutual deed of indemnity with the holding company. The company must supply sufficient information to allow preparation of group accounts.

Local audits do not differ from IFAC guidelines.

Austria.

An annual audit is required for

- All "Aktiengesellschaften" (joint stock companies)
- "Gesellschaften mit beschrankter Haftung" (limited liability companies), in case at least two of the three following criteria are exceeded for three years:
  —balance sheet total of ATS 200 million
  —annual turnover of ATS 300 million
  —annual average of 300 employees
- Limited liability companies with a supervisory board; a supervisory board is compulsory i.e. for all capital investment companies, and for companies with a nominal capital exceeding ATS 1 million and more than 50 shareholders.
- Commercial partnerships, whose sole unlimitedly liable partner is a company (joint stock or limited liability company) requiring a statutory audit itself. In this case the criteria listed above relate to the partnership as a whole.

Barbados.

All public companies as well as private companies incorporated under the Barbados Companies Act with gross revenues or assets exceeding Bds$ 1 million are subject to a GAAS audit.

Special rules apply to offshore companies as these are regulated under certain other statutes which take precedence over the Companies Act. International business companies require an audit where their gross revenues or assets exceed Bds$ 1 million. Offshore banks and exempt insurance companies are required to have an audit but foreign sales corporations are exempt.

Belgium.

An annual GAAS audit is required by law. Exemption is granted if, on a consolidated basis, the group to which the company belongs does not exceed more than one of the following three criteria:

- turnover BF 178 million
- balance sheet total of BF 75 million or
- average employees 50.

Appointment of statutory auditors must be approved by the Workers' Council.

Local audits do not differ from IFAC guidelines.

Brazil.

Statutory audits in Brazil are only required for quoted companies and financial institutions (e.g. commercial banks, investment banks). Quoted companies (including quoted financial institutions) are also subject to quarterly reviews by independent accountants.

Canada.

In Canada, incorporation may be achieved through the provisions of either the federal Canada Business Corporations Act or the corresponding legislation of one of the ten Canadian provinces. Generally a statutory audit is required, but there are exemptions for small companies which have not offered securities to the public in Canada. Under the federal legislation, a small company is considered to be one with less than Can$10 million in revenue and less than Can$5 million in assets. Under the Ontario act, the corresponding parameters are Can$5 million in revenue and Can$2.5 million in assets. In addition, in some jurisdictions, such as Ontario, exemptions may be granted to companies over the size parameters if it can be demonstrated that the applicant is not economically significant in Canada and that granting the exemption will not be contrary to public interest.

Cayman Islands.

The only statutory audit requirements in the Cayman Islands relate to banks and trust companies and insurance companies licenced under the relevant local legislation. Audits must be performed in accordance with International, US, Canadian or UK auditing standards. Any other form of MNC subsidiary is therefore not subject to statutory audit.

Chile.

Compulsory requirements for GAAS audits of annual financial statements apply to entities subject to surveillance by control agencies (principally Superintendency of Corporations and Superintendency of Banks).

Companies that:

- quote their shares in the local stock exchange,
- have issued marketable bonds,
- have a large number of shareholders, or
- voluntarily become subject to the control mechanisms established by current regulations, are subject to surveillance by the Superintendency of Corporations.

Although not directly controlled by this agency, the financial statements of subsidiaries of these corporations should comply with the accounting regulations of the Superintendency and should file audited accounts. Insurance companies, insurance brokers, certain investment funds, mutual funds and other specific entities are also subject to control by the Superintendency of Corporations. Banks are subject to control by the Superintendency of Banks. All other corporations are exempted from this surveillance but may be required to file audited accounts in certain instances (e.g. under special foreign investment regulations).

Statutory audits are also normally required for purposes of remitting dividends abroad by other entities.

Colombia.

Statutory audits are required for Colombian companies and other companies with share capital and for branches of foreign corporations. There are no exemptions from this requirement.

Local statutory auditors are required, not only to issue a report on the examination of financial statements under rules which do not significantly differ from IFAC guidelines, but also to:

- Report whether adequate internal control rules exist and have been observed;
- Report on compliance with legal regulations (including instructions from official surveillance agencies), company bylaws, instructions of the board of directors and decisions of the shareholders or partners in general meeting;
- Report on the proper handling of correspondence, minutes of meetings, shareholder registers, etc.; and
- Report (to management, shareholders or official surveillance agencies, as the case may be) on irregularities and internal control weaknesses when they occur, and issue instructions to the persons whose duty is to correct them.

The above duties involve of course a continuous audit of operations and the permanent assessment of compliance with internal and external regulations.

Denmark.

An annual GAAS audit is required by law and there are no exemptions.

Local audits do not differ from IFAC guidelines.

El Salvador.

Statutory audits have to be performed by a duly registered Salvadoran CPA.

A full scope audit is required by law for all corporations, national and foreign.

Finland.

An annual GAAS audit is required by law and there are no exemptions.

Local audits significantly differ from IFAC guidelines and local competitors may perform less than a full scope audit. Because of public criticism of audits of some major companies, introduction of stricter accounting legislation and auditing standards is in process.

France.

An annual GAAS audit is required by law. Exemption is granted for limited liability companies (SARL) and General Partnership (SNC) which do not meet two of the following three criteria:

- a balance sheet total of FF 10 million
- a turnover of FF 20 million
- 50 employees

Local auditing norms are very similar to IFAC guidelines. It is possible that some smaller firms do not apply such norms.

Gabon.

A statutory auditor must be appointed for each limited liability company (i.e. with a turnover over FCFA 400 million). The statutory auditor must be registered with the local institute of accounting experts.

Germany.

An annual GAAS audit is required by law for limited liability companies other than small companies as well as for large sole proprietorships and partnerships. Small companies are those which do not exceed two of the following three criteria:

- balance sheet total DM 3.9 million
- net sales DM 8 million
- annual average of 50 employees.

Local GAAS do not differ from IFAC guidelines and audit scopes are generally equal to a US or UK GAAS audit.

Greece.

All companies that meet a certain size test are required to be audited by a government body (SOL). Precise scope of a SOL audit is not known but appears to be a GAAS audit with an emphasis on compliance. All other smaller companies require a statutory audit, but in practice, non-SOL auditors carry out virtually no audit work.

Hong Kong.

An annual GAAS audit is required by law for all companies incorporated in Hong Kong and there are no exemptions for this requirement.

Local audits do not differ from IFAC guidelines.

India.

Statutory audit required under the Indian Companies Act envisages the following:

- Full scope GAAS audit
- Verification of certain additional information required to be disclosed under the Companies Act (refer to appendix XI, Doing Business in India)
- Performance of certain additional checks for compliance with Maocaro (a type of long form) reporting requirements (refer to chapter 11—pages 92–95, Doing Business in India)

Ireland, Northern.

Full scope audit required for all limited companies in accordance with the Companies (Northern Ireland) Order 1986.

Ireland, Republic of.

A statutory audit is required for all companies and the auditor is required to report on the true and fair view and a number of other matters which must be reported in all cases.

Italy.

An annual GAAS audit is required by law for selected companies (quoted companies, insurance companies, state-owned companies etc.) and there are no exemptions from this requirement. Such local audits are not less stringent than those required under IFAC guidelines.

Jamaica.

Under the Jamaican Companies Act, an audit is required for all locally incorporated companies and branches of overseas companies. Audited financial statements have to be filed with the Registrar of Companies.

A statutory audit is a full scope audit in accordance with GAAS and must be performed by an auditor licensed under the Public Accountancy Act.

There are no exemptions to the above.

Japan.

The Commercial Code requires a corporation (kabushiki kaisha) to have at least one statutory auditor (kansayaku). This person may not be a company employee, and professional qualifications are not necessary. The financial documents subject to the statutory auditor's opinion are the balance sheet, the income statement, proposals relating to the distribution of profit or loss, supplementary account statements, and the report on the business.

If a corporation has paid-in capital of at least 500 million yen or total liabilities of 20 billion yen or more (referred to as a large corporation), the Commercial Code requires that financial documents of the corporation be audited by a member of the Japanese Institute of Certified Public Accountants (JICPA). The appointment of auditor(s) must be approved at the general shareholders' meeting with the consent of a majority of the statutory auditors.

Korea.

The joint stock company of which total asset exceeds 4 billion Won as at the end of its previous fiscal year is subject to the audit by a licensed external (independent) auditor.

The audit examination must be in accordance with generally accepted audit standards established by the Securities Management Committee (SMC in Korea can be compared to the SEC of the USA) with the approval of the Ministry of Finance.

Mexico.

An annual statutory audit is required for all corporations. In addition, tax compliance audits are required for all companies or groups of companies meeting any one of the three size criteria, currently (1992):

- gross income in excess of Ps 5 850 million,
- total assets in excess of Ps 11 700 million, or
- more than 300 employees. Most subsidiaries of MNCs fall into this category.

While the scope of the statutory audit is similar to IFAC guidelines, the tax compliance audit involves additional detailed reporting and audit documentation representing, on average, 35% more audit hours than a GAAS audit, in order to satisfy the requirements of the tax authorities.

Morocco.

A statutory audit is required for Moroccan corporations. However, the law does not set auditing and reporting standards. In practice local statutory auditors limit their scope to the reconciliation of the accounting records to the financial statements and issue a variety of opinions.

The statutory audit law is in the process of being changed.

Namibia.

All companies registered in Namibia require an audit.

All branches of foreign companies that operate in Namibia require a statutory audit.

GAAS audit requirements are currently the same as for the Republic of South Africa (refer to the Doing Business Guide for South Africa).

The Netherlands.

All companies other than those classified by the law as small require a statutory audit. Small companies are those which do not exceed two of the following three criteria:

- balance sheet total DFIs 5 million
- turnover DFIs 10 million
- annual average 50 employees

Exemption possibilities exist where the Dutch subsidiary's parent company, being subject through applicable law to the EC 7th Directive, guarantees the indebtedness of the Dutch company.

A company with subsidiaries is generally required to present consolidated accounts as well as parent company accounts. The company may be exempted from the consolidated presentation where it is part of a larger group and the group accounts conform to the standards promulgated by the IASC.

New Zealand.

The members of private companies and those which have less than 25% foreign control can elect not to appoint an auditor. All other companies must have an annual audit.

Local audits do not differ from IFAC guidelines.

Nicaragua.

Statutory audits are required for foreign investments registered with the Central Bank in order to be able to remit profits and/or dividends.

Statutory audits have to be performed by a duly registered Nicaraguan CPA.

Statutory audit is not required for national investors, except for their income tax return preparation.

Norway.

An annual GAAS audit is required by law. Companies with a turnover of NOK 2 million or less are exempted.

Local audits do not differ from IFAC guideline.

Papua New Guinea.

A statutory audit is required for all companies except for exempt proprietary companies. An exempt proprietary company can generally be defined as a proprietary company in which no share is beneficially owned directly or indirectly by a public company. Papua New Guinea branches of foreign companies do not require a separate audit.

Statutory audits in Papua New Guinea are conducted in accordance with International Auditing Guidelines. The local Accountants Association has adopted all the International Accounting Standards and its members are encouraged to ensure that these standards are adopted in the preparation of financial statements.

Peru.

An annual GAAS audit is required by law for the following entities:

- companies making public stock offerings registered in the stock exchange or requesting registration and quotation in the exchange.

- companies with annual gross revenues over a certain amount (US$ 400 000).
- companies that apply for credit from a public or private banking or financial institution.

Philippines.

An annual GAAS audit is required by law and there are no criteria for exemption.

Local audits do not differ from IFAC guidelines.

Portugal.

All Sociedades Anonimas are required to have a statutory audit, as are Limitadas that exceed two of the following parameters:

- total assets Esc 180 million,
- total income Esc 370 million, or
- 50 employees.

Statutory auditing standards are deemed to be in accordance with IAG and the audit report makes specific reference to "true and fair." Statutory audits may be carried out by qualified sole practitioners or statutory auditing firms registered with the local institute. No international firm is currently registered. As there is no effective quality control, statutory audits by local firms and practitioners are often not carried out in accordance with IAG.

Puerto Rico.

Puerto Rico tax law contains specific statutory audit requirements for companies engaged in business in Puerto Rico. These requirements specify that the audits must be conducted in accordance with US generally accepted auditing standards (GAAS). In addition, the resulting financial statements must be prepared using US generally accepted accounting principles (GAAP) for attachment to various Puerto Rico tax filings. The statutory financial statements must be certified by a CPA licensed in Puerto Rico.

Saudi Arabia.

All limited liability companies and corporations (including foreign subsidiaries and branches) are required to submit audited accounts certified by a registered public accountant in Saudi Arabia. They are also required to file their audited accounts with the Department of Zakat (Income Tax). Moreover, all limited liability subsidiaries where foreign investment is involved have to file annual audited accounts with the Ministry of Industry and Electricity. Such companies are also required to maintain Arabic books of account and records in the Kingdom.

Singapore.

An annual GAAS audit is required by law and there are no exemptions.

Local audits do not differ from IFAC guidelines. However, for entities in the financial services sector (particularly banks), a statutory audit involves extended scope and reporting because of the regulatory requirements of the Monetary Authority of Singapore.

South Africa.

All companies (defined to include branches of foreign companies) must have their annual financial statements audited by a registered public accountant and auditor. Close corporations are exempt.

The scope of the work necessary for an auditor to express an opinion is a full scope examination which must be carried out in accordance with generally accepted auditing standards in South Africa. These are essentially the same as US, UK and IFAC standards.

Spain.

An annual GAAS audit is required by law for all limited liability companies which exceed two of the following conditions for two consecutive years:

- Net turnover of 480 million Pesetas,
- Total assets of 230 million Pesetas, or
- Average number of employees during the year of 50.

Local audits do not significantly differ from IFAC guidelines.

Sweden.

An annual GAAS audit is required by law and there are no exemptions.

Local audits do not differ from IFAC guidelines.

Switzerland.

An annual audit is required by law. The auditor must be qualified. In certain circumstances the auditor must be specially qualified. (The definition of these terms, qualification and special qualification, has not yet been published.) Nonetheless it is still possible that GAAS are not observed.

A specially qualified auditor is required if the company:

- has bonds in issue
- has issued shares which are quoted or traded on a stock exchange
- fulfills certain size criteria (balance sheet total SFr 20 million, turnover SFr 40 million, an average of 200 employees).

The statutory auditor must be independent, have a place of business in Switzerland and be recorded in the Commercial Register.

Taiwan.

The law requires annual GAAS audits of banks, insurance companies and trust companies; quoted companies (semi-annually) and other companies whose issued capital or bank loans exceed NT$ 30 million.

In addition to the above some other companies must have their annual tax return audited. Specific audit scopes are presented for such audits, including the requirement that each expense caption be tested for 15% of value.

Tanzania.

Statutory audit requirements in Tanzania are:

- Compliance with Local and International Accounting and Auditing Standards
- Compliance with companies ordinances and other relevant legislation.

Thailand.

GAAS statutory audit is required. Statutory accounts are to be submitted to the Ministry of Commerce and to accompany income tax returns.

Trinidad & Tobago.

All companies incorporated under the Companies Ordinance require to be audited independently. The Institute of Chartered Accountants of Trinidad & Tobago has established that all members must conduct audits in accordance with "approved auditing standards" which are the IFAC guidelines. No exemptions exist based on size but branches of non-resident companies are not governed by the above prescriptions.

A new Companies Ordinance is being drafted which, if enacted, will allow for smaller companies to dispense with an audit.

Turkey.

Only banks and quoted companies have statutory audit requirements in the international sense and these call for a full GAAS audit.

United Kingdom.

An annual GAAS audit is required by law. An exemption from this requirement is available for inactive subsidiaries.

Local audits do not differ from IFAC guidelines.

United States.

An annual audit is required if a company has publicly traded debt or equity securities. In addition, banks or others lending frequently require audited financial statements on an annual basis.

Audits are conducted in accordance with US GAAS.

Uruguay.

Local legislation requires that statutory audits be performed for:

- Financial institutions; which are subject to close Central Bank surveillance are required to submit, in addition to their audited financial statements, other audited information such as a detailed categorization of risks and related allowances for loan losses and an auditor's report on the fair compliance with Central Bank standards of the information provided during the year to the Central Bank.
- Public transportation companies; which under Montevideo city council regulations, are required to submit, in addition to their audited financial statements, audited bus ticket cost information and related projections—as a basis for fixing bus rates.
- Companies held by the National Corporation for Development; a government entity that groups a wide range of investments in the private sector.
- Companies required to file their financial statements with public entities; which must enclose a compilation report prepared by a certified public accountant.

Venezuela.

An annual GAAS audit is not required by law. However, for foreign companies a GAAS audit is required for filing with superintendent of foreign investments. There are no exemptions.

Local audits do not significantly differ from IFAC guidelines. Local competitors would perform little audit work.

Zaire.

There is no legal requirement for a GAAS audit.

Zimbabwe.

A statutory audit of a private company is required in Zimbabwe where:

- the number of shareholders exceeds 10; or
- a public corporation is a shareholder; or
- a private company is a shareholder, which in turn is a subsidiary of a public corporation; or
- a private company is a shareholder, which in turn is a subsidiary of a holding corporation that has itself appointed auditors.

CHAPTER 10

CORPORATE FINANCIAL DATA FOR INTERNATIONAL INVESTMENT DECISIONS

Frederick D.S. Choi

New York University

SUPPLEMENT CONTENTS

10.3 GLOBAL DATA BASE SURVEY.

Page 10 · 8, replace Wright Investors Service *in second column of last entry of Exhibit 10.1 with:*

Lotus Development Corp.

CHAPTER **11**

GLOBALIZATION OF WORLD FINANCIAL MARKETS: PERSPECTIVE OF THE U.S. SECURITIES AND EXCHANGE COMMISSION

Sara Hanks

Rogers & Wells

SUPPLEMENT CONTENTS

11.3 HOW THE SEC AFFECTS INTERNATIONAL ACCOUNTING STANDARDS.

Page 11 · 7, add at end of first full paragraph:

The IASC issued three exposure drafts dealing with these changes and has received comments on those. Final decisions are yet to be made with respect to these issues.

11.4 CHALLENGES POSED TO THE SEC BY INTERNATIONAL DEVELOPMENTS.

Page 11 · 8, add at end of second full paragraph:

This report has since been updated (most recently to reflect regulations in force in September 1991).

* *Page 11 · 9, add at end of fourth paragraph:*

Over the last two years, the SEC has substantially liberalized its position on the application of its stabilization and antimanipulation rules in the context of international offerings. Many such offerings, particularly Rule 144A offerings of securities traded in a non-U.S. market that the SEC considers as providing adequate protection to investors, are now exempted from the application of these rules without the need to obtain a no-action letter.

Page 11 · 14, add after first full paragraph:

The system was adopted in May 1991. Despite commenters' negative reaction to the reconciliation requirement for offerings of securities other than investment-grade debt and preferred stock, the reconciliation requirement was retained for two years following adoption of the system, at the end of which it will lapse unless the SEC takes affirmative action to retain it.

11.5 THE COMMISSION'S RESPONSE TO GLOBALIZATION.

° *Page 11 · 15, final paragraph third line, delete "investors" and replace with:*

specified institutional buyers

° *Page 11 · 15, final paragraph, delete language in parentheses and replace with the following:*

certain types of securities are excluded from the $100 million

SOURCES AND SUGGESTED REFERENCES

Page 11 · 17, add in alphabetical order:

International Equity Offerings: Changes in Regulation since April, 1990 International Organization of Securities Commissions, September 1991.

Multijurisdictional Disclosure and Modifications to the Current Registration and Reporting System for Canadian Issuers, Securities Act Release No. 6902, June 21, 1991.

CHAPTER 13

INTERNATIONAL ACCOUNTING STANDARDS AND ORGANIZATIONS: QUO VADIS?

Arthur R. Wyatt

Arthur Andersen & Co. and International Accounting Standards Committee

SUPPLEMENT CONTENTS

13.5 OUTLOOK FOR INCREASED HARMONIZATION.

Page 13 · 18, and new subsection:

(d) Alternative Harmonization Scenarios (New).   At least two possible harmonization scenarios can be identified. One involves the notion of bilateral (or mutual) agreements. Under this approach, two (or more) countries negotiate for mutual recognition of each other's standards. Sometimes the agreement will call for certain additional disclosures or reconciliations to satisfy conditions for mutual recognition. However, if the demands of this nature by any party become significant, agreement on mutual recognition is unlikely. That is, unless the differences between countries' standards are relatively few, the disclosures or reconciliations become both burdensome and difficult to understand.

This mutual recognition approach has a surface attraction, but has significant practical difficulties. The process of evolving a bilateral agreement, generally at the governmental level, is very time consuming and can involve considerations that are really not germane to fairness in financial reporting. The objective is to gain acceptance of each other's filing scheme in limited circumstances. Thus, the major beneficiaries are the securities regulators, not the users of the financial information who would continue to be faced with financial information prepared under multiple sets of accounting standards. Financial statement users do not benefit, but regulators have overcome barriers to cross-border trading of securities at a cost of perpetuating noncomparability of available financial information.

Another scenario flows more directly from the initiatives in process at IASC. Agreements are achieved on professional issues at an international level of representatives of national accounting professions. These agreements reflect emerging international trade and capital market initiatives and, to succeed, must also reflect standards that are of top quality and not simply lowest common denominators. The standards must reflect a sufficiently high level of quality that the regulators can feel comfortable accepting them and then promoting them within their individual country government structures. This approach benefits from the private sector expertise and has promise for success if all the participants, both private sector and government, continue to work together in a realistic partnership.

CHAPTER 14

HARMONIZATION OF AUDITING STANDARDS

Robert N. Sempier
International Federation of Accountants (Retired)

Roy A. Chandler
Cardiff Business School

Anthony N. Dalessio
International Federation of Accountants

SUPPLEMENT CONTENTS

14.3 STRUCTURE OF IFAC.

Page 14 · 4, replace second sentence of first paragraph with:

At present, 106 accounting bodies in 78 countries comprise the membership of IFAC.

Page 14 · 4, replace the word guidelines *in first sentence of last paragraph with* standards.

Page 14 · 5, replace the word guidelines *in first sentence of second paragraph with* pronouncements.

14.5 THE ROLE OF IAPC.

Page 14 · 6, replace first paragraph following the heading with:

IAPC has responsibility for developing and issuing standards on generally accepted auditing practices and on related services. To date it has issued approximately 30 International Standards on Auditing and four Standards on Related Services.

Page 14 · 6, replace the word guideline *in fifteenth line with* standard.

Page 14 · 6, replace the word guideline *in nineteenth line with* standard.

Page 14 · 6, replace the acronym IAG *in twenty-sixth line with* ISA (International Standard on Auditing).

Page 14 · 6, replace the word guideline *in twenty-eighth line with* standard.

Page 14 · 6, replace the acronym IAGs *in thirtieth line with* ISAs.

Page 14 · 7, replace the word guidelines *in first line of first full paragraph with* standards.

Page 14 · 7, replace the acronym IAGs *in first two sentences of second full paragraph with* ISAs.

Page 14 · 7, replace the words international auditing guidelines *in first sentence of third full paragraph with* international standards on auditing.

Page 14 · 7, replace the word guidelines *in second sentence of third full paragraph with* standards.

* *Page 14 · 7, before fourth full paragraph, insert:*

At its October 1992 Conference, IOSCO endorsed the ISAS FASB. In making this announcement, it stated that the ISAS represent a comprehensive set of auditing standards, and audits conducted in accordance with these standards could be relied upon by securities regulatory authorities for multinational reporting purposes.

This endorsement would have the effect of encouraging all members to accept the FSAs as an acceptable basis for use in cross-border offerings and continuous reporting by foreign issues. In addition, IOSCO recommends that its members take all steps that are necessary and appropriate in their home jurisdictions to accept and conducted in accordance with ISAs or an alternative to domestic audit standards in connection with cross-border offerings and continuous reporting by foreign issues.

Page 14 · 7, replace fourth full paragraph with:

At present, international standards on auditing do not override national auditing regulations. IFAC has no enforcement powers. However, IFAC encourages its member bodies to

- Adopt international standards on auditing as their own (especially in countries that do not have their own standards).
- Compare their standards to international standards on auditing and seek to eliminate any material differences (in countries that have their own standards).
- Persuade relevant authorities in their country of the benefits of harmonization with international standards on auditing (in countries where the framework of auditing practice is contained in law).

* *Page 14 · 7, after the sentence ending in "contained in law":*

In 1992, IAPC started working on its Codification and Improvements project.

14.8 THE FUTURE.

Page 14 · 10, replace the word guidelines *in first sentence of second full paragraph with* pronouncements.

Page 14 · 10, replace the acronym IAG *in second sentence of second full paragraph with* ISA.

* *Page 14 · 10, add at the end of section 14.8:*

14.9 OTHER IFAC PUBLICATIONS.   *Statement of Policy of IFAC Council: Assuring the Quality of Audit and Related Services.* This statement of policy discusses the steps that can be taken to enhance quality control within accounting firms.

Study: Impact of Information Technology on the Accountancy Profession. In recognition of the impact of information technology (IT) on the accountancy profession, IFAC established a Task Force whose terms of reference included the requirement to undertake a broad-ranging study of the likely impacts of advances in IT on the education and work of accountants and on the role and structure of the accountancy profession. This study details the findings and recommendations of the Task Force.

IFAC Towards the 21st Century: Strategic Directions for the Accountancy Profession. The Statement discusses the mission of IFAC.

International Capital Markets Group Publications.

SOURCES AND SUGGESTED REFERENCES

Page 14 · 11, replace the word Guidelines *in seventh reference with:* Standards.

* *Page 14 · 11, add after the eleventh reference:*

————, *IFAC Towards the 21st Century: Strategic Directions for the Accountancy Profession.* New York: IFAC, 1992.

* *Page 14 · 11, replace fourteenth reference with:*

International Standards on Auditing 1–30. New York: IFAC, January 1980–February 1992.

Page 14 · 11, replace fifteenth reference with:

————, *International Standards on Auditing/Related Services Guidelines 1–4.* New York: IFAC, February 1988–October 1990.

* *Page 14 · 11, add after the fifteenth reference:*

————, *International Education Discussion Paper.* New York: IFAC, September 1992.
————, *International Capital Markets Group Publications.* New York, London: IFAC, IBA, 1991–1992.

* *Page 14 · 11, replace sixteenth reference with:*

International Education Guidelines 1–18. New York: IFAC, February 1982–November 1991.

Page 14 · 11, delete seventeenth reference.

Page 14 · 11, replace eighteenth reference with:

————, *International Code of Ethics for Professional Accountants.* New York: IFAC, July 1992.

* *Page 14 · 11, replace nineteenth reference with:*

International Management Accounting Practices 1–5. New York: IFAC, February 1989–October 1991.

Page 14 · 11, replace twenty-first reference with:

———, *International Public Sector Guidelines 1–3.* New York: IFAC, July 1989–February 1992.

* *Page 14 · 11, add after the twenty-first reference:*

———, *International Public Sector Study 1.* New York: IFAC, March 1991.

Page 14 · 11, replace twenty-third reference with:

———, *Preface to International Standards and Statements on Auditing of the International Federation of Accountants.* New York: IFAC, July 1989.

* *Page 14 · 11, replace twenty-fourth reference with:*

———, *Proposed International Standards on Auditing 1–30.* New York: IFAC, July 1, 1992.

Page 14 · 11, delete twenty-fifth reference.

* *Page 14 · 11, add after twenty-fifth reference:*

———, *Statement of Policy of IFAC Council, Assuring the Quality of Audit and Related Services.* New York: IFAC, July 1992.
———, *Study, Impact of Information Technology on the Accountancy Profession.* New York: IFAC, October 1992.

* *Page 14 · 11, replace twenty-sixth reference with:*

———, *Summary of International Standards on Auditing and Related Services (ISAs 1–30 and ISA/RSs 1–4).* New York: IFAC, March 31, 1991.

APPENDIX A

EDUCATION COMMITTEE

Page 14 · 13, add before the period at end of title for IEG numbers 1, 3, and 4–6:

(Consolidated into Guideline 9)

Page 14 · 13, add before the period at end of title for IEG 8 title:

(Consolidated into Guideline 9)

Page 14 · 14, add after IEG 8:

IEG 9: Prequalification Education, Tests of Professional Competence and Practical Experience of Professional Accountants. This guideline provides a framework for the education and training which all professional accountants should acquire to become qualified. (The preceding IEGs 1, 3, 4–6, and 8 have been consolidated into IEG 9.)

* *IEG10: Professional Ethics for Accountants: The Educational Challenge and Practical Application.* The Federation recommends that member bodies review their arrangements for the education of their members and future members in the area of professional ethics, an area vital to the public perception of the accounting profession.

* *Discussion Paper: Specialization on the Accounting Profession.* The purpose of this paper is to encourage discussion with member bodies on the question of specialization in the accounting profession. The paper outlines some trends and forces that are operating to lead the profession towards specialization, to suggest possible approaches to the question, and discusses some of the advantages and disadvantages associated with formal specialization.

ETHICS COMMITTEE

Page 14 · 14, replace first line of second full paragraph with:

International Code of Ethics for Professional Accountants. This code sets forth

Page 14 · 15, delete third bullet.

Page 14 · 15, delete last paragraph (SGE 12).

Page 14 · 16, add after last sentence in "Practice No. 3":

Practice No. 4: Management Control of Projects. This statement describes the management control of projects, as contrasted with the management control of ongoing operations.

* *Practice No. 5: Managing Quality Improvements.* This guideline provides practical operating principles and recommended approaches for implementing total quality management. It is addressed to management accountants so they can fully employ their unique skills in the quality management process.

EXPOSURE DRAFTS (EDs)

Page 14 · 16–17, delete Exposure Drafts 4–6.

INTERNATIONAL AUDITING PRACTICES COMMITTEE

Page 14 · 17–22, replace the following subsections:

Preface to International Auditing Guidelines and Statements on Auditing.
Framework of International Guidelines on Auditing and Related Services.
International Auditing Guidelines (IAGs).
International Auditing Guidelines/Related Services—(IAG/RSs).

with:

Preface to International Standards on Auditing and Statements on Auditing. The Preface explains the modus operandi of IAPC in developing its pronouncements and the relative authority attaching to ISAs and International Statements on Auditing. There is also specific reference to the need to comply with the applicable IFAC ethical guidance when conducting audits under ISAs.

Framework of International Standards on Auditing and Related Services. Standards are issued in two separate series, auditing (ISAs) and related services (ISA/RSs) which comprise reviews, agreed-upon procedures and compilations. The Framework describes the services that auditors may be engaged to perform in relation to the resulting level of assurance. Audits and reviews are designed to enable the auditor to provide high and moderate levels of assurance, respectively, that information is free of material error. In an agreed-upon procedures engagement, the auditor reports the factual findings of performing procedures which have been agreed with his client but he does not express any assurance on assertions. In a compilation engagement, the auditor uses his accounting expertise to collect, classify and summarize financial information but he does not express any assurance on assertions. The Framework also discusses the circumstances in which an auditor may accept a change in the terms of an engagement and auditor association with client financial information.

ISA 1: Objective and Basic Principles Governing an Audit.   The Standard describes management's responsibility for financial statements and the overall objective and scope of the audit of financial statements of an entity by an independent auditor. This Standard describes the basic principles governing an auditor's professional responsibilities which should be exercised whenever an audit is carried out. The basic principles identified involve: integrity, objectivity and independence, confidentiality, skills and competence, work performed by others, documentation, planning, obtaining audit evidence, reviewing accounting systems and internal control, reviewing conclusions reached, and reporting. These basic principles are the cornerstone of all succeeding International Standards on Auditing.

ISA 2: Audit Engagement Letters.   An auditor's engagement letter to the client is designed to document and confirm the auditor's acceptance of the appointment, the scope of the auditor's work, and the extent of the auditor's responsibilities and the form of any reports. The Standard describes the principal contents of an engagement letter, and the appendix contains an example of a letter.

ISA 4: Planning.   The guidance applies to the planning process of the audit of both financial statements and other financial information. It is framed in the context of recurring audits, identifies key elements in the planning process and provides practical examples of items which should be considered when planning an audit. Adequate audit planning helps to ensure that appropriate attention is devoted to important areas of the audit, that potential problems are promptly identified, and that the work is completed expeditiously. Planning also assists in proper utilization of assistants and in coordination of work done by other auditors and experts.

ISA 5: Using the Work of an Other Auditor.   The auditor's considerations to be made when intending to use the work of another auditor are described. The guidance applies when an independent auditor reporting on the financial statements of an entity uses the work of another independent auditor with respect to the financial statements of one or more divisions, branches, subsidiaries or associated companies included in the financial statements of the entity. For the purposes of this Standard, offices of the principal auditor's firm in a different country, affiliated firms, correspondents, and unrelated auditors who are involved in the audit of components of the entity are considered as other auditors.

ISA 6: Risk Assessment and Internal Control.   The purpose of this Standard is to provide guidance to the auditor in obtaining an understanding of and testing the internal control system; and assessing inherent and control risks, and using such assessments to design substantive procedures which the auditor intends to perform in order to restrict detection risk to an acceptable
* level. Addendum 1 to ISA 6 discusses the EDP characteristics and considerations. Addendum 2 to ISA 6 discusses audit considerations relating to entities using service organizations.

ISA 7: Control of the Quality of Audit Work.   Controlling the quality of audit work is essential in maintaining the high standards of the profession. This Standard distinguishes between controls on individual audits and general quality controls adopted by an audit firm. While recognizing the interrelationship of the two types of controls, general quality controls "augment and facilitate" controls on individual audits but do not replace them. Controls over delegation of work to assistants on an individual audit in order to comply with the basic auditing principles are addressed, and practical assistance is provided to an audit firm in controlling the general quality of their practice. An appendix with examples of procedures is provided to assist a firm in implementing quality control policies.

ISA 8: Audit Evidence.   Audit evidence is information obtained by the auditor in arriving at the conclusions upon which an opinion on the financial information is based. The nature and sources of audit evidence are described as well as the sufficiency and appropriateness of audit evidence and the methods by which it is obtained by the auditor in the performance of compliance and substantive procedures.

ISA 8 Addendum 1: Additional Guidance on Observation of Inventory, Confirmation of Accounts Receivable and Inquiry Regarding Litigation and Claims.   Guidance is provided on the application of audit evidence gathering procedures (attendance at stocktaking, direct confirmation of accounts receivable and direct communication with a client's lawyers) that are generally accepted as providing the most reliable audit evidence in relation to certain assertions. The Addendum outlines the circumstances when these procedures should be applied and the matters to be considered in their implementation. Observation of inventory is required (unless impracticable) when inventories are material to the financial statements in order to obtain evidence of the physical existence and condition of inventory. Confirmation of accounts receivable is required when accounts receivable are material, and provides evidence of the existence of debtors and the accuracy of recorded balances. Guidance is given on the selection of accounts to be confirmed, the use of positive and negative confirmations and the use of alternative procedures when confirmation is inappropriate or replies to confirmations contain exceptions. Direct communication with the entity's lawyer is required when litigation or claims have been identified or are believed may exist. Guidance is given on the form and content of the communication, and the need for the auditor to consider meetings with the lawyer if matters are complex or there is a disagreement.

* **ISA 8 Addendum 2: Additional Guidance on Long-Term Investments and Segment Information.**   Guidance is provided on the auditing procedures the auditor should carry out in order to provide a reasonable basis to conclude on these items.

ISA 9: Documentation.   Guidance is provided on the general form and content of working papers as well as specific examples of working papers normally prepared or obtained by the auditor. Ownership and custody of working papers is also discussed.

ISA 10: Using the Work of an Internal Auditor.   The internal audit function constitutes a separate component of internal control undertaken by specially assigned staff within an entity. An objective of the internal auditor is to determine whether internal controls are well designed and properly operated. Much of the work of the internal audit department may be useful to the independent auditor for the purpose of his examination of the financial information. Guidance is provided as to the procedures that should be considered by the independent auditor in assessing the work of the internal auditor.

ISA 11: Fraud and Error.   This Standard defines fraud and error, and indicates that the responsibility for the prevention of fraud and error rests with management. The auditor should plan the audit so that there is a reasonable expectation of detecting material misstatements resulting from fraud and error. Suggested procedures are provided which should be considered when the auditor has an indication that fraud or error may exist. An appendix sets out examples of conditions or events which increase the risk of fraud or error.

ISA 12: Analytical Procedures.   A description of the nature of analytical review procedures is provided as well as guidance on the objectives, timing and extent of reliance to be placed on such procedures in performing an audit. Also discussed is the auditor's investigation of unusual fluctuations.

ISA 13: The Auditor's Report on Financial Statements.   Guidance is provided to auditors on the form and content of the auditor's report issued in connection with the independent audit of the financial statements of an entity. The Standard includes suggested wording to express an unqualified opinion and discusses circumstances that may result in other than an unqualified opinion. An appendix sets forth examples of an unqualified, qualified, and adverse auditor's reports and a denial of opinion.

ISA 14: Other Information in Documents Containing Audited Financial Statements.   This Standard defines "other information" as financial and non-financial information included in a document which contains an entity's audited financial statements together with the auditor's report thereon. An entity usually issues such a document on an annual basis which is frequently referred to as the "annual report". In certain circumstances, the auditor has a statutory obligation to report on other information and in other circumstances he has no such obligation. This guidance discusses the auditor's consideration of other information on which he has no obligation to report and the actions he should undertake if a material inconsistency or material misstatement of fact is discovered.

ISA 15: Auditing in an EDP Environment.   Guidance is provided to auditors on the additional procedures necessary to comply with ISA 3, "Basic Principles Governing an Audit," when auditing in an EDP environment. The skills and competence required of the auditor are described as well as his responsibility when he delegates such work to assistants or uses work performed by others.

ISA 16: Computer-Assisted Audit Techniques.   This Standard provides guidance to the auditor when using computer-assisted audit techniques (CAATs)—particularly audit software and test data. The ISA outlines instances when CAATs may be used, factors to consider in determining whether to use a CAAT and the major steps to be performed in CAAT application. In addition, special considerations when using CAATs in a small business computer environment are highlighted.

ISA 17: Related Parties.   Discussed are the procedures to be considered in obtaining sufficient appropriate audit evidence concerning the existence of and transactions with related parties. This Standard is premised on the definition and disclosure requirements set out in International Accounting Standard (IAS) 24, "Related Party Disclosures." ISA 17 provides guidance to assist auditors in determining whether management of an entity has properly disclosed related party relationships and transactions with such parties in accordance with the provisions of IAS 24.

ISA 18: Using the Work of an Expert.   This Standard provides guidance to the auditor in instances when using the work of an expert (specialist) engaged or employed by the client or auditor. The ISA outlines examples of cases when an auditor may need to use the work of an expert and provides guidance on considerations relating to the expert's skills, competence and objectivity. ISA 18 outlines considerations that should be made by the auditor for communicating with the expert and offers specific guidance on evaluating the work of an expert.

ISA 19: Audit Sampling.   The factors that an auditor should consider when designing and selecting an audit sample and evaluating the results of audit procedures are identified. The ISA applies to both statistical and nonstatistical sampling methods and provides fundamental yet practical guidance on such matters as sampling risk, stratification, selection methods, and projection of errors.

ISA 21: Date of the Auditor's Report; Events After the Balance Sheet Date; Discovery of Facts After the Financial Statements Have Been Issued.   Guidance is provided on dating of the auditor's report; the auditor's responsibility in relation to subsequent events, which are significant events occurring after the balance sheet date, and the auditor's responsibility in connection with the discovery of facts after the financial statements have been issued. This Standard describes steps the auditor generally performs to identify subsequent events, responsibilities in relation to events after the date of the auditor's report but before the financial statements are issued, and discovery of facts after the financial statements are issued. An appendix sets forth an example of an auditor's report on revised financial statements.

ISA 22: Representations by Management.   This Standard provides guidance to the auditor on using management representations as audit evidence, procedures the auditor should apply in evaluating and documenting them, and circumstances in which written representations should be obtained. It indicates that with regard to representations for material financial statement matters, the auditor should seek corroborative evidence, evaluate the representations for reasonableness and consistency with other audit evidence and other representations, and consider whether the individual making the representation can be expected to be well-informed. It also notes that representations can be documented in the working papers by summarizing oral discussions or by obtaining written representation. The Standard also notes the conditions for obtaining a letter from management and considerations of the auditor when management refuses to provide or confirm representations on matters considered necessary.

ISA 23: Going Concern.   Guidance is provided to auditors in discharging their responsibilities in situations in which the appropriateness of the going concern assumption as a basis for the preparation of financial statements is in question. The Standard notes that an entity's continuance as a going concern is assumed in the absence of information to the contrary. If this assumption is unjustified, an entity may not be able to realize its assets at the recorded amounts and there may be changes in the amount and dates of maturity of liabilities resulting in the need for financial statements to be adjusted. ISA 23 provides examples of indications that continuance as a going concern should be questioned, outlines the standards for collecting audit evidence when such a question arises, and describes the audit procedures that may be performed to obtain such evidence. In addition, it sets out the auditor's reporting considerations in such circumstances.

ISA 24: Special Purpose Auditor's Reports.   This Standard provides guidance to auditors that issue audit reports that are other than those covered by ISA 13, notably, (a) financial statements prepared in accordance with a comprehensive basis of accounting other than international accounting standards or relevant national standards; (b) specific accounts, elements of accounts, or items of financial statements; (c) compliance with contractual agreements; and (d) summarized financial statements. Appendices contain illustrations of special purpose auditor's reports.

ISA 25: Materiality and Audit Risk.   This Standard defines the concepts of materiality and audit risk, their interrelationship and the application of these concepts by an auditor when planning and conducting an audit and evaluating the results of his procedures. Materiality is defined as the magnitude or nature of a misstatement including an omission of financial information either individually or in the aggregate that, in the light of surrounding circumstances, makes it probable that, as a result of the misstatement, the judgment of a reasonable person relying on the information would have been influenced or his decision affected. The assessment of materiality is a matter of the auditor's professional judgment and is considered at both an overall level and in relation to individual account balances and disclosures. Audit risk is defined as the risk that an auditor may give an inappropriate opinion of financial information that is materially misstated. Audit risk is considered at the financial statement level and the account balance and class of transactions level. The three components of audit risk are discussed and their interrelationship explained. An appendix illustrates this interrelationship.

ISA 26: Audit of Accounting Estimates. Guidance is provided to auditors on the audit procedures that should be performed in order to obtain reasonable assurance as to the appropriateness of accounting estimates contained in financial information. An accounting estimate is defined as an approximation of the amount of an item in the absence of a precise means of measurement. It is noted that management is responsible for making accounting estimates based upon its judgment of the uncertain outcome of events that have occurred or are likely to occur and that the auditor is responsible for evaluating the reasonableness of such estimates. ISA 26 sets out the main steps involved in the audit of accounting estimates and provides the auditors with guidance on the evaluation of errors in accounting estimates. It is stated that, due to the approximation inherent in accounting estimates, such an evaluation can be made more difficult than in other areas of the audit.

ISA 27: The Examination of Prospective Financial Information. This Standard deals with the examination and reporting procedures where an auditor is asked to report on prospective financial information being either a forecast, based on best-estimate assumptions, or a projection based on hypothetical assumptions. Recognizing the future oriented nature of the engagement, the examination procedures recognize the speculative nature of the evidence available to the auditor, and while acknowledging a consistent audit objective, differentiates between the evidence requirements and process for best-estimate as distinct from hypothetical assumptions. Emphasis is given to the importance of adequate disclosure of significant assumptions to an understanding of prospective financial information and the auditor's role in ensuring this occurs. It is noted that an auditor cannot obtain a high level of assurance that the information is free of material misstatement, but that a useful service can be provided by providing a moderate level of assurance as to whether the assumptions provide a reasonable basis for the prospective financial information, and an opinion as to whether the information has been properly prepared on the basis of the assumptions. A statement cautioning readers that the auditor is not providing an opinion as to whether the results shown in the projected information will be achieved is also recommended. Appendices illustrate reports on a forecast and a projection.

ISA 28: First Year Audit Engagements—Opening Balances. This Standard provides guidance as to the auditor's responsibilities for opening balances when the financial statements are being audited for the first time or were audited by another auditor in the prior year. The ISA outlines the audit procedures by which sufficient appropriate audit evidence may be obtained in both circumstances to determine whether the opening balances were misstated, correctly brought forward or restated and appropriate accounting policies consistently applied. The auditor's reporting considerations are set out where the auditor is unable to obtain sufficient appropriate audit evidence and where the prior year audit report was other than unqualified. Appendices contain illustrations of other than unqualified reports.

* **ISA 30: Knowledge of the Business.** This standard sets out what is meant by a knowledge of the business, why it is important to the auditor and to members of the audit staff working on an engagement, why it is relevant to all phases of an audit and how the auditor obtains and uses that knowledge.

INTERNATIONAL STANDARDS ON AUDITING/RELATED SERVICES (ISA/RSs)

ISA/RS 1: Basic Principles Governing Review Engagements. ISA/RS 1 is a parallel document to ISA 3, Basic Principles Governing an Audit, setting out the basic principles and general and reporting guidelines for review engagements. A review engagement is defined as an engagement in which an auditor is asked to carry out procedures which provide a moderate level of assurance on financial information, being a lower level of assurance than that provided by an audit. A review consists primarily of procedures that involve inquiry and analytical review. The specific objective of a review is to give the auditor an appropriate basis for stating whether anything has come to his attention that causes him to believe that the information does not give a true or fair view (or "is not presented fairly") in accordance with the basis of accounting indicated. The style of reporting used is known as negative assurance and is clearly distinguishable from an audit opinion.

ISA/RS 2: Review of Financial Statements. This Standard describes the procedures the auditor should consider when engaged to review financial statements and the form of the content of the report to be issued. The procedures, consisting primarily of inquiry and analytical review, are performed to provide the auditor with a reasonable basis for stating whether anything has come to his attention that causes him to believe that the financial statements do not give a true and fair view (or "are not presented fairly") in accordance with the basis of accounting indicated. A sample engagement letter and a listing of common review engagement procedures are set forth in appendices.

ISA/RS 3: Engagements to Perform Agreed-Upon Procedures. This Standard describes the basic principles and general guidelines to be followed when an auditor is engaged to apply procedures, which the auditor and client have agreed on, to individual items of financial data, a financial statement or set of financial statements. Guidance is also given on the types of procedures that may be applied and the form and content of the report of factual findings to be issued. As the procedures are agreed between the auditor and client to meet the client's needs for particular information, it is suggested that the auditor meet with the client and other specified parties who will receive copies of the report to ensure there is a clear understanding of the nature, purpose and extent of the engagement and procedures to be applied. Furthermore, the auditor is only required to present the evidence collected to the user, and the report of factual findings provides no assurance on assertions. Appendices illustrate a sample engagement letter and report of factual findings including an illustrative list of procedures.

ISA/RS 4: Engagements to Compile Financial Information. This Standard describes the basic principles and general guidelines to be followed when an accountant undertakes an engagement to compile financial information, the types of procedures that should be applied and the form and content of the accountant's report. The guidance is based on the auditor using his accounting rather than auditing expertise. The guidance requires that the accountant ensure there is a clear understanding between the client and accountant regarding the nature and extent of the engagement. While there is no requirement for the accountant to test the assertions underlying the information, the accountant should obtain a knowledge of the business and operations of the client, the accounting and reporting principles and practices of the industry and the nature of the entity's business transactions. While the accountant is required to consider whether compiled information is free from obvious misstatement, the procedures are not designed and are not sufficient to enable the auditor to express any assurance. Appendices illustrates a sample engagement letter and compilation reports.

Page 14 · 23–24, delete Exposure Drafts 32–35.

PUBLIC SECTOR COMMITTEE

Page 14 · 24, replace International Auditing Guidelines *in title of last paragraph with* International Standards on Auditing.

Page 14 · 24, replace IAGs *in last paragraph with* ISAs.

Page 14 · 24, add after the last paragraph:

International Public Sector Guideline No. 3: Applicability of International Standards on Auditing to the Audit of Financial Statements of Governments and Other Non-Business Public Sector Entities.   This guideline sets out the applicability of ISAs to the audit of financial statements of public sector entities other than government business enterprises.

* *Study No. 1: Financial Reporting by National Governments.*   This study identifies the objectives of the financial reports of national governments and their major units, and examines the degree to which those objectives are met by different bases of accounting and reporting models. The study looks at the general purpose financial reports of national governments and their major units. Although focused on national governments, it may also be relevant to financial reporting by state, provincial, regional, and local governments.

CHAPTER 15

CONSOLIDATED FINANCIAL STATEMENTS AND JOINT VENTURE ACCOUNTING

Benjamin S. Neuhausen
Arthur Andersen & Co.

SUPPLEMENT CONTENTS

15.5 ACCOUNTING FOR INVESTMENTS IN SUBSIDIARIES.

(b) Required Accounting for Investments in Subsidiaries.

* *Page 15 · 10, replace subsection (ii) Canada with the following:*

The primary guidance in Canada is Section 1590 of the *CICA Handbook*. Section 1590 defines a subsidiary as "an enterprise controlled by another enterprise (the parent) that has the right and ability to obtain future economic benefits from the resources of the enterprise and is exposed to the related risks." Control of an enterprise is defined as:

> the continuing power to determine its strategic operating, investing and financing policies without the co-operation of others . . . . An enterprise is presumed to control another when it owns, directly or indirectly, an equity interest that carries the right to elect the majority of the members of the other enterprise's board of directors, and is presumed not to control the other enterprise without such ownership.

Control does not exist if an enterprise is acquired "with the clearly demonstrated intention that it be disposed of in the foreseeable future." In addition, control does not exist, even when one enterprise has majority voting rights in a second enterprise, if a statute or agreement imposes "severe long-term restrictions" on the ability of the second enterprise to distribute earnings to the first enterprise or undertake other transactions with the first enterprise. "For example, the imposition of severe foreign exchange or currency export restrictions over a foreign subsidiary may indicate that control has been lost."

A parent should fully consolidate all subsidiaries. Certain disclosures are required if an enterprise concludes that it does not control another enterprise despite ownership of majority voting rights or concludes that it does control another enterprise despite not owning majority voting rights.

* *Page 15 · 10, add the following at the end of the first paragraph in subsection (iii) European Community:*

All member states have now conformed their local requirements to the Seventh Directive. It is currently effective in all member states except Italy, where it will become effective for fiscal years ending on or after April 30, 1994.

* *Page 15 · 12, replace the last two sentences of the first paragraph in subsection (iv) United Kingdom:*

The accounting requirements are contained in Accounting Standards Committee SSAP No. 1, "Accounting for Associated Companies," as amended by Accounting Standards Board Interim Statement, "Consolidated Accounts," and by Accounting Standards Board FRS 2, "Accounting for Subsidiary Undertakings."

* *Page 15 · 13, replace third sentence of item 1 with the following:*

FRS 2 states that "cases of this sort are so exceptional that it would be misleading to link them in general to any particular contrast of activities. For example, the contrast between Schedule 9 and 9A companies (banking and insurance companies and groups) and other companies or between profit and not-for-profit undertakings is not sufficient of itself to justify non-consolidation."

* *Page 15 · 13, replace references to ED 50 in items 2, 3, 4 with* FRS2.

* *Page 15 · 13, replace references to ED 49 in second complete paragraph with the following:*

Accounting Standards Board Financial Reporting Exposure Draft (FRED) 4, "Reporting the Substance of Transactions."

* *Page 15 · 13, add the following at the end of the first paragraph of subsection (v) Japan:*

These materiality rules regarding the scope of consolidation are being reexamined by the Ministry of Finance and JICPA.

(d) Exclusion of Subsidiaries from Full Consolidation.

* *Page 15 · 16, replace the second sentence of subsection (iii) with the following:*

The trend is clearly in favor of full consolidation, with the United States, Canadian, and IASC rules requiring consolidation regardless of line of business, and the United Kingdom interpreting the exclusion narrowly.

CHAPTER 19

EMPLOYERS' ACCOUNTING FOR PENSION COST

James R. Ratliff

New York University

SUPPLEMENT CONTENTS

19.1 INTRODUCTION.

° *Page 19 · 2, delete section and replace with following:*

(a) Scope.   This chapter deals with accounting for pension costs and liabilities for pension benefits and other postretirement benefits reported in the financial statements of an employer. It also includes a discussion of the settlement and curtailment of pension plans and other postretirement benefits. It does not deal with employment termination indemnities, deferred compensation, or long-service leave benefits.

An employer may undertake the responsibility for pensions and other postretirement benefits, either voluntarily or by law. Accounting for these benefits and the recognition of a liability may differ under different circumstances.

The responsibility for retirement benefits may be either detailed in a written plan or in an oral or implied agreement. If it is a written agreement, the plan may be either funded or unfunded. If it is a funded plan, the fund generally will be administered by trustees. When a fund is present, the amount required to be paid into the fund in a particular fiscal period may differ from the amount of expense that needs to be recorded on the books of the sponsoring employer. The objective of funding is to ensure that funds are available to pay the benefits when they are due. It is a financing procedure. On the other hand, the objective of accounting for the cost of a plan is to ensure that the cost of the benefits are allocated to the accounting periods in which the employee gives the service, in a systematic manner. The calculation of the amount to be funded will not be discussed.

This chapter will concentrate on accounting for pensions and other postretirement benefits under the rules of Financial Accounting Standard (FAS) No. 87, *Employers' Accounting for Pensions,* (FAS) No. 88, *Employers' Accounting for Settlements and Curtailment of Defined Benefit Pension Plans and for Termination Benefits,* (FAS) No. 106, *Employers' Accounting for Postretirement Benefits Other Than Pensions,* and International Accounting Standard (IAS) No. 19, *Accounting for Retirement Benefits in the Financial Statement of Employers.* In addition, it will review the accounting for such cost and liabilities in various countries where these rules are not followed.

(b) Background.   Pension and other postretirement cost are often a major portion of an employer's compensation package. It is, therefore, important that they be accounted for properly and that appropriate disclosures be made in the financial statements of the employer.

(i) Defined Benefit Versus Defined Contribution Plan.   Pension plans may be either defined benefit plans or defined contribution plans. A "defined benefit plan" can be a pension plan that defines the amount of pension benefit to be provided to an employee at retirement. The amount of the contribution, to be made by the sponsor of the plan, is determined actuarially, based on benefits expected to be paid. A "defined contribution plan" can be a plan that specifies the amount of contribution that is to be made by the employer, but not the amount of the benefits to be paid. The amount of the benefits to be paid depends on the amount contributed to the participants' individual accounts, the returns earned on the investment of those contributions, and forfeiture of other participants' benefits that may be allocated to such participants' accounts.

Accounting for defined contribution plans is generally easier than accounting for defined benefit plans. The net pension cost for a defined contribution plan is the required contribution for the period to the extent that the contribution is made in the period in which the employee renders service. There is generally no other liability incurred.

(ii) Government Plans.   As discussed in International Accounting Standard (IAS) No. 19, some employers are required to make payments into national or state benefit plans. If the plans

are not the responsibility of the employer but rather of the government and, if the cost of the plan is assessed on all of the employers in the country, it would be appropriate to record the expense as the service is rendered and the money paid into the fund.

(c) Actuarial Valuation Methods. The 1981 FASB Discussion Memorandum, "Employers Accounting for Pensions and Other Postemployment Benefits," described two families of attribution approaches: benefit approaches and cost approaches. IAS No. 19 uses the terms "accrued benefit valuation methods" and "projected benefit valuation methods" to describe these same terms.

In the benefit approach, the amount of pension benefits attributed to a period is determined, and then the service cost component for the period as the actuarial present value of those benefits is calculated. As described in FAS No. 87, the "cost approach projects an estimated total benefit at retirement and then calculates the level contribution that, together with return on assets expected to accumulate at the assumed rates, would be sufficient to provide that benefit at retirement. (The amount allocated to each year may be level in dollar amount or level as a percentage of compensation.)"

Cost approaches, or projected benefit valuation methods, include the following actuarial methods: The entry age normal method, the individual-level premium method, the aggregate method, and the attained-age normal method.

19.2 ACCOUNTING FOR DEFINED BENEFIT PENSION COSTS AND LIABILITIES IN THE UNITED STATES.

Page 19 · 4, insert before subsection (a):

Definitions

(i) Single Employer Plan.   A postretirement plan that is maintained by one employer or by related parties, such as a parent and its subsidiary.

(ii) Multi-employer Plan.   A postretirement plan to which two or more unrelated employers contribute, usually pursuant to a collective bargaining agreement. The assets contributed by one employer may be used to provide benefits to employees of other participating employers. The plan is usually administered by a joint board of trustees, composed of management and labor representatives.

(iii) Projected Benefit Obligation.   The actuarial present value as of a specified date of all benefits attributed by the pension plan formula to employee service rendered prior to that date.

(iv) Accumulated Benefit Obligation.   The actuarial present value of benefits attributed by the pension benefit formula to employee services rendered before a specific date and based on employee service and compensation (if applicable) prior to that date.

(v) Vested Benefit Obligation.   The actuarial present value of the vested benefits.

(vi) Vested Benefits.   The benefits for which the employee's right to receive present or future pension benefits is no longer contingent on remaining in the service of the employer.

(vii) Final Pay Plans.   A defined benefit pension plan that promises benefits based on an employee's compensation at or near retirement. The benefits may be based on the last year's compensation or on an average of a number of years specified in the plan.

* *Page 19 · 26, add new section:*

19.7A EMPLOYERS' ACCOUNTING FOR POSTRETIREMENT BENEFITS OTHER THAN PENSIONS (NEW).

(a) Definitions.

(i) Postretirement Benefits Other Than Pensions.   All forms of benefits other than retirement income provided by an employer to retirees, beneficiaries, or covered dependents. Benefits may be defined in terms of specified benefits, such as health care, tuition assistance, or legal services, that are provided to retirees as the need for those benefits arise, or they may be defined in terms of monetary amounts that become payable on the occurrence of a specified event, such as life insurance benefits.

(ii) Expected Postretirement Benefit Obligation.   The actuarial present value as of a particular date of the benefits expected to be paid to or for an employee, the employee's beneficiaries, and any covered dependents pursuant to the terms of the postretirement benefit plan. It is equivalent to the total benefit obligation in pension accounting.

(iii) Accumulated Postretirement Benefit Obligation.   The actuarial present value of benefits attributed to employee service rendered to a particular date. Prior to an employee's full eligibility date, the accumulated postretirement benefit obligation as of a particular date for an employee is the portion of the expected postretirement benefit obligation attributed to that employee's service rendered to that date; on and after the full eligibility date, the accumulated and expected postretirement benefit obligations for an employee are the same. This would correspond to the projected benefit obligation under pension accounting.

(iv) Full Eligibility Date.   The date at which an employee has rendered all of the service necessary to have earned the right to receive all of the benefits expected to be received by that employee (including any beneficiaries and dependents expected to receive benefits).

(v) Per Capita Claims Cost.   The current cost of providing postretirement health care benefits for one year at each age from the youngest age to the oldest age at which plan participants are expected to receive benefits under the plan.

(vi) Health Care Cost Trend Rate.   An assumption about the annual rate of change in the cost of health care benefits currently provided by the postretirement benefit plan, due to factors other than changes in the composition of the plan population by age and dependency status, for each year from the measurement date until the end of the period in which benefits are expected to be paid. The trend rate implicitly includes such factors as inflation, changes in the health utilization rates, or patterns and technology advances.

(b) Funding Policies.   Most postretirement benefits other than pensions are not funded in the United States. There is no law requiring funding of postretirement benefits other than pensions, and the expense is not deductible for tax purposes until the benefits are actually paid. Thus funding would require the outlay of cash without any corresponding reduction in the income tax obligation.

(c) Fundamentals of Accounting for Postretirement Benefits Other Than Pensions.   The fundamentals of accounting for postretirement benefits are basically the same as those for accounting for pensions as set forth in FAS No. 87; i.e., the delayed recognition of certain events such as past service cost, transition amounts and gains and losses. The recognition of postretirement costs as a single net amount is composed of six components: (1) service cost, (2) interest

cost, (3) expected return on plan assets, (4) amortization of past service cost, (5) amortization of gains and losses, and (6) the amortization of the unrecognized net obligation or unrecognized net asset existing at the date or initial application of FAS No. 106 (transition amount).

(d) Measurement of Cost and Obligation.   Any measurement of the cost and obligations of a postretirement benefit plan must take into consideration the substantive plan, the estimates or assumptions made about future events and an attribution approach that assigns benefits and the cost of those benefits to individual years of service.

(i) Accounting for the Substantive Plan.   The written plan provides the best evidence of the terms of the agreement between employer and employees. The substantive plan may differ from the written plan in the area of cost-sharing policy and the practice of regular increases in monetary benefits. If the substantive plan differs from the written plan, the substantive plan is the basis for accounting.

Cost-sharing policy, as evidenced by following past practice or communication, constitutes the cost-sharing provisions of the substantive plan if either of the following conditions exist. The employer has a past practice of (1) maintaining a consistent level of cost sharing between the employer and retires through a change in deductibles, coinsurance provisions, retiree contributions, or some combination of these; (2) consistently increasing or reducing the employer's share of the cost of the covered benefits through changes in the contribution of the retired or active plan participants. If the employer has not in the past had a cost-sharing policy, but has the ability and has communicated to affected plan participants its intent to institute different cost-sharing provisions at a specified time or when certain conditions are met, the cost-sharing policy is considered to be part of the substantive plan.

A past practice of regular increases in postretirement benefits defined in terms of monetary amounts may indicate that the employer has a present commitment to make future improvements to the plan. In those circumstances, the substantive commitment to increase those benefits should be the basis for accounting.

(ii) Assumptions.   FAS 106 requires that all assumptions made in the calculation of the postretirement benefit cost be explicit. They must be reasonable, and the best assumptions that can be made taking into consideration the current plan participants and the current plan including any amendments that have been made but not yet put into effect. Some of these assumptions are the same as those that must be made in connection with the determination of net pension cost. Others are unique to postretirement health care benefits.

Assumptions that must be made include the selection of a discount rate and an expected long-term rate of return on plan assets (if the plan has assets). Assumptions must also be made relating to the probability of payment, including turnover, retirement age, dependency status, and the mortality rate.

In addition to these, other assumptions unique to postretirement health care must be made, such as per capita claims cost by age and the health care cost trend rate.

(iii) Attribution.   An equal amount of the expected postretirement benefit obligation for an employee will generally be attributed to each year of service in the attribution period; i.e., a benefit/years of service approach. The attribution period begins on the day the employee is hired unless the plan's benefit formula grants credit only for service from a later date, in which case the attribution period will begin on that latter date. The end of the attribution period is the full eligibility date.

(e) Recognition of Net Periodic Postretirement Benefit Cost.   The net periodic postretirement benefit cost consists of six components: service cost, interest cost, actual return on plan assets (if any), amortization unrecognized prior service cost, amortization of gains and losses, and amortization of the unrecognized transition obligation or unrecognized transition asset.

(i) Service Cost.   The service cost component of net periodic postretirement benefit cost is that portion of the expected postretirement benefit obligation (EPBO) attributed to employee service during a period. If an employee is hired at age 25 and the full eligibility for the benefit is reached at age 55, then the service cost each year for this employee would be calculated by multiplying $1/30$ times the EPBO. If an EPBO of $30,000 is assumed, the service cost component would be $1,000, since the employee is expected to work 30 years from the date of hire to the full eligibility date.

(ii) Interest Cost.   The interest cost component of postretirement benefit cost is the accrual of interest on the accumulated postretirement benefit obligation due to the passage of time. It would be calculated by multiplying the accumulated postretirement benefit obligation (APBO) by the discount rate. Therefore if a discount rate of 10 percent and an APBO of $10,000 is assumed, the interest cost component would be $1,000.

(iii) Expected Return on Plan Assets.   The expected return on plan assets is calculated by multiplying the market-related value of plan assets by the expected long-term discount rate. The difference between the expected return and actual return on plan assets for the period would be disclosed as a deferred gain or loss and would be recognized on a delayed basis. As discussed earlier, most postretirement benefit plans are not funded so generally the expected return on plan assets would be zero.

(iv) Amortization of Prior Service Cost.   Prior service cost is the cost of retroactive benefits from plan initiation or amendments. It is measured as the change in the APBO based on the APBO measured before the change in benefits and after the change in benefits. This change is accounted for prospectively; immediate recognition of the cost is not permitted.

In the case of pensions, because of ERISA, prior service cost always results in an increase in the PBO. However in the case of other postretirement benefits, an amendment to a plan may result in either an increase or decrease in the APBO. The accounting for an increase and the accounting for a decrease in the APBO is not the same. Prior service cost resulting from an amendment that increases APBO is amortized over the remaining years of service of active participants to the full eligibility date of each plan participant active at the date of the amendment who was not fully eligible for benefits at that date, or for the expected period to be economically benefited, if shorter. Another method of amortization may be used as long as the resulting amortization is not less than the required method and if it is applied consistently. This would generally mean a straight-line method based on the average remaining service period to the full eligibility date.

Service cost resulting from a plan amendment that decreased the APBO would (1) reduce unrecognized prior service cost, (2) reduce any remaining unamortized transition obligation, and (3) would be amortized the same as an increase in the APBO. For an illustration of the method of amortization of a service cost that was brought about by an increase in the APBO, refer to the section on net pension cost.

(v) Amortization of Gains and Losses.   Gains and losses are defined as the change in the value of either the accumulated postretirement benefit obligation (APBO) or plan assets resulting from experience different from that assumed or a change in the assumption. Gains and losses include amounts that have been realized (for example, the sale of a security), as well as amounts that are unrealized. Gains and losses are not normally required to be recognized in the year they occur. Gains and losses are measured the same as under FAS No. 87.

As a minimum, any unamortized net gain or loss present at the beginning of the year must be amortized if it exceeds 10 percent of the greater of (a) the accumulated postretirement benefit obligation, or (b) the market-related value of the plan assets. If amortization is required, the minimum amortization will be that excess divided by the average remaining service period of active plan participants. This method of amortization is known as the corridor approach and is illustrated in the section on pensions.

Any systematic method of amortization of the unrealized net gain or loss may be used in place of the corridor approach provided that (a) the minimum amortization is recognized in any period in which it is greater than the amount that would be recognized under the corridor approach, (b) the method is used consistently, (c) the method is applied similarly to both gains and losses, and (d) the method used is disclosed.

An enterprise may also use a method of consistently recognizing gains and losses immediately. If this method is used, any gain that does not offset a loss previously recognized in income must first offset any unrecognized transition obligation. Any loss that does not offset a gain previously recognized in income must first offset any unrecognized transition asset.

(vi) Transition Asset or Obligation.   The transition obligation is defined as the unrecognized amount, as of the date the statement is initially applied, of the accumulated postretirement benefit obligation in excess of the fair value of plan assets plus any recognized accrued postretirement benefit cost or less any recognized prepaid postretirement benefit cost. A transition asset is defined as the unrecognized amount as of the date the statement is initially applied of the fair value of plan assets plus any recognized accrued postretirement benefit cost or less any recognized prepaid postretirement benefit cost in excess of the accumulated postretirement benefit obligation. It is rare for an entity to have a transition asset.

The transition amount, whether an asset or an obligation, may be recognized immediately in the net income of the period of the change as the effect of a change in accounting principles or on a delayed basis as a component of net periodic postretirement benefit cost.

If delayed recognition of the transition asset or obligation is selected, it shall be amortized over the remaining service period of the active employees. However, if the average remaining service period is less than 20 years, the transition amount may be amortized over 20 years. It must be amortized more quickly if the cumulative benefit payments subsequent to the transition to all plan participants exceed the cumulative postretirement benefit cost accrued subsequent to the transition date. If this occurs, an additional amount of the unrecognized transition obligation must be recognized equal to the excess cumulative benefit payments.

(f) Illustration of Implementation of FAS No. 106 and the Calculation of Postretirement Benefit Cost.   The following is an illustration of the implementation of FAS No. 106 including the determination of the accumulated postretirement benefit obligation and the net periodic postretirement cost. The net postretirement benefit cost will be determined the same way each year. The example also illustrates the reconciliation of the funded status of the net periodic postretirement benefit cost.

Company XYZ adopts FAS No. 106 on January 1, 1993. The postretirement benefit plan includes a provision that all employees are fully eligibile to receive benefits on reaching the age of 55. The Company determines that the discount rate is 10 percent and that the transition obligation will be amortized over a 20-year period.

Employees	Status	Current Age	Age Hired	Expected Age at Retirement	EPBO	APBO
Jane	Active	35	25	55	$ 9,000	$ 3,000
Joe	Active	50	30	62	12,500	10,000
Ann	Active	60	35	65	14,000	14,000
John	Retired	70	30	N/A	8,000	8,000
Total						$35,000

The APBO is a portion of the EPBO until the full eligibility date. The APBO is calculated by dividing the difference between the current age less the date hired by the difference between the full eligibility date and the date hired and then multiplying by the EPBO. For Jane that would be

$$\frac{35-25}{55-25} \times 9,000 = 3,000$$

Assuming no changes in the plan and the discount rate of 10 percent, the EPBO at the end of the year would be calculated as follows:

Employees	EPBO 1/1/93	Interest	Benefit Payments	EPBO 12/31/93
Jane	$ 9,000	$ 900	N/A	$ 9,900
Bill	12,000	1,200	N/A	13,750
Ann	14,000	1,400	N/A	15,400
John	8,000	800	(400)	8,400

The APBO of 12/31/93 will reflect the impact of the passage of time through the accrual of service cost and interest cost for one year as well as benefit payments made during the year as follows:

Employees	APBO 1/1/93	Service Cost (a)	Interest Cost (b)	Benefit Payments	APBO 12/31/93
Jane	$ 3,000	$330	$ 300	N/A	$ 3,630
Bill	10,000	550	1,000	N/A	11,550
Ann	14,000	N/A	1,400	N/A	15,400
John	8,000	N/A	800	(400)	8,400
Total	$35,000	$880	$3,500	$(400)	$38,980

(a) The service cost component of net periodic postretirement benefit cost is calculated for only the participants that have not reached the full eligibility date. It is calculated as follows:

Employees	Attribution Period	EPBO 12/31/93	Fraction Attributed to First Year	Service Cost
Jane	30	$ 9,900	1/30	$330
Bill	25	13,750	1/25	550
				$880

(b) The interest cost component is calculated for all participants whether or not they have reached full eligibility date or have retired it is calculated as follows:

Employees	APBO 1/1/93	Interest at	Interest Cost
Jane	$ 3,000	10%	$ 300
Bill	10,000	10%	1,000
Ann	14,000	10%	1,400
John	8,000	10%	800
Total	$35,000		$3,500

If we assume for simplicity that the plan is unfunded and that since statement No. 106 was adopted in 1993, there would be no gain or loss amortization or no prior service cost amortization, the net post periodic postretirement cost for the year would be:

Service cost	$ 800
Interest cost	3,500
Actual return on plan assets	0
Amortization of transition obligation over 20 years ($35,000/20)	1,750
	$6,130

The funded status of the plan is reconciled to the accrued postretirement benefit cost at the beginning and end of the year as follows:

Reconciliation of Funded Status Net Periodic Postretirement Benefit Cost

	Actual 1/1/93	Service Cost	Interest Cost	Amortization of Transition Obligation	Benefit Payments	Actual 12/31/93
Accumulated postretirement benefit obligation	−35,000	−880	−3,500	0	400	−38,980
Plan assets	$0.00	0	0	0	0	0
Funded status	−35,000	−880	−3,500	0	400	−38,980
Unrecognized net (gain) or loss	0	0	0	0	0	0
Unrecognized prior service cost	0	0	0	0	0	
Unamortized transition obligation	35,000	0	0	−1,750	0	33,250
Accrued postretirement benefit cost	0	−880	−3,500	−1,750	400	−5,730

(g) Illustration of the Calculation of the Estimated Postretirement Benefit Obligation. To determine the EPBO, you must first calculate the assumed per capita claims cost and then calculate the EPBO. In this illustration, it is assumed that a participant is 50 years old, expects to retire at the end of the year in which he turns 62, and will commence receiving benefits at the age of 63. His life expectancy is 70. A 12 percent health care trend rate and a 7 percent discount rate is assumed. The assumed per capita claims cost would be determined as follows:

Determining the Per Capita Claims Cost

Age	1992 per Capita Claims Cost	Health Care Cost Trend Rate of 12% Applied for	Future Health Care Cost	Medicare and Other Third-Party Reimbursement	Applied per Capita Claims Cost
63	$ 950.00	13 years	$ 4,145.00	$ 0.00	$ 4,145.00
64	1,000.00	14 years	4,887.00	0.00	4,887.00
65	1,065.00	15 years	5,829.00	4,722.00	1,107.00
66	1,204.00	16 years	7,380.00	5,830.00	1,550.00
67	1,290.00	17 years	8,857.00	7,047.00	1,810.00
68	1,365.00	18 years	10,496.00	7,926.00	2,570.00
69	1,442.00	19 years	12,420.00	9,812.00	2,608.00
70	1,595.00	20 years	$15,386.00	$12,463.00	2,923.00
Total					$21,600.00

The per capita claims cost is the average cost for a participant at each age. The future health care cost is calculated by the use of the future value of 1 for each year the participant is expected to receive benefits. The applied per capita claims cost is then calculated by subtracting the amounts expected to be received from medicare or other third-party reimbursements. The medicare reimbursements is based on current laws and regulations.

The Expected Postretirement Benefit Obligation can now be calculated. To calculate the EPBO the assumed per capita claims cost is discounted at the present value of 1 at 7 percent (the discount rate).

Measuring the Expected Postretirement Benefit Obligation

Age	Assumed per Capita Claims Cost	Discount Rate of 7% Applied for	Present Value at Age 50
63	$4,145.00	13 years	$1,720.00
64	4,887.00	14 years	1,895.00
65	1,107.00	15 years	401.00
66	1,550.00	16 years	525.00
67	1,810.00	17 years	573.00
68	2,570.00	18 years	760.00
69	2,608.00	19 years	721.00
70	$2,923.00	20 years	755.00
Total			$7,350.00

19.7B SETTLEMENTS AND CURTAILMENTS OF OTHER POSTRETIREMENT BENEFITS (NEW).

(a) Settlement of Postretirement Benefit Obligations.   Three criteria must be met to have a settlement of a postretirement benefit obligation: (1) a settlement must be a transaction that is irrevocable, (2) it must relieve the employer (or plan) of primary responsibility for the postretirement benefit obligation, and (3) it must eliminate significant risks related to the obligation and assets used to effect the settlement.

(b) Accounting for Settlement of the Postretirement Benefit Obligation.   The maximum gain or loss to be recognized in the income statement is the unrecognized net gain or loss since transition plus any remaining unrecognized transition asset. The maximum gain or loss includes any gain or loss resulting from remeasurement of plan assets and the accumulated postretirement benefit obligation at the time of the settlement.

If the entire accumulated postretirement benefit obligation is settled, and there is a settlement gain the gain must first reduce any remaining unrecognized transition obligation and then the excess is included in income. If there is a settlement loss, the maximum settlement loss will be recognized in income. If only a part of the accumulated postretirement benefit obligation is settled, the employer should recognize in income the excess of the pro rata portion of the maximum settlement gain over any remaining unrecognized transition obligation or a pro rata portion of the maximum settlement loss.

The following illustration demonstrates the accounting for a settlement of a postretirement benefit obligation when an unrecognized transition obligation exists.

In the example that follows, Company X sponsors a postretirement life insurance plan. On January 1, 1993, the company adopted FAS No. 106. On December 31, 1994, Company X settles the APBO for its current retires ($35,000) through the purchase of nonparticipating life insurance contracts. At December 31, 1994, the cumulative postretirement benefit cost accrued subsequent to the date of transition exceeds the cumulative benefit payments subsequent to that date. The results of the settlement are as follows:

	December 31, 1994		
	Before Settlement	Settlement	After Settlement
Accumulated postretirement benefit obligation	$(128,500)	$ 35,000	$(93,500)
Plan assets at fair value	36,500	(35,000)	1,500
Funded status	$ (92,000)	0	$(92,000)
Unrecognized net gain	(22,288)	6,062	(16,226)
Unrecognized prior service cost	16,500		16,500
Unrecognized transition obligation	97,500	(6,602)	91,438
Accrued postretirement benefit cost	$ (228)	0	$ (228)

The maximum settlement gain subject to recognition is the unrecognized net gain subsequent to transition plus any unrecognized transition asset in this case $22,288. Since only part of the APBO is settled there must be a pro rata allocation ($35,000/$128,500 = 27.2%). That amount ($22,288 × 27.2%) must first reduce any unrecognized transition obligation, any excess is then recognized in income. In this case, no income is to be recognized.

(c) Curtailment of a Postretirement Benefit Obligation.   A curtailment is an event that significantly reduces the expected years of future service of active plan participants or eliminates the accrual of defined benefits for some or all of the future services of a significant number of active participants. Examples of curtailments include closing of a facility, discontinuing a segment of the business, or downsizing.

(d) Accounting for a Curtailment.   The unrecognized prior service cost associated with the portions of future years of service expected to be rendered but, as a result of the curtailment, are no longer expected to be rendered is a curtailment loss. For the purpose of determining the curtailment loss, prior service cost includes any unrecognized transition obligation.

As part of a curtailment, the accumulated postretirement benefit obligation may be decreased (a gain) or increased (a loss). That gain or loss will reduce any unrecognized net gain or loss (a) to the extent that such gain exceeds any unrecognized net loss, it is a curtailment gain, and (b) to the extent that such a loss exceeds any unrecognized net gain, it is a curtailment loss. Any remaining unrecognized transition asset will be treated as an unrecognized net gain and will be combined with the unrecognized net gain or loss arising subsequent to transition.

If there is a net curtailment loss, it will be recognized in income when it is probable that a curtailment will occur and the net effect is reasonably estimable. If there is a net curtailment gain, it will be recognized in income when the related employees terminate or the plan suspension or amendment is adopted.

(e) Illustration of a Curtailment Gain.   An example of a curtailment when an unrecognized gain and an unrecognized transition obligation exist follows.

Company Z sponsors a postretirement benefit plan. On November 30, 1995, Company Z decides to reduce its operations by terminating a significant number of employees effective December 31, 1995. On November 30, it is expected that a curtailment will result from the termination. The remaining years of expected service associated with those terminated employees who were plan participants at the transition is 22 percent of the remaining years of service of all plan participants at the date of transition. The remaining years of service prior to full eligibility associated with the terminated employees who were plan participants at the date of a prior plan amendment is 18 percent of the remaining years of service of all plan participants at the date of the plan amendment.

	December 31, 1995		
	Before Curtailment	Curtailment	After Curtailment
Accumulated postretirement benefit obligation	$(128,500)	$27,000	$(101,500)
Plan assets at fair value	36,500		36,500
Funded status	92,000	27,000	(65,000)
Unrecognized net gain	(22,288)		(22,288)
Unrecognized prior service cost	16,500	(2,970)	13,530
Unrecognized transition obligation	97,500	(21,450)	76,050
(Accrued) prepaid postretirement benefit cost	$ (288)	$ 2,580	$ 2,292

The curtailment gain consists of two components. (1) The unrecognized transition obligation associated with the remaining years of service no longer expected to be rendered. That is 22 percent of the unrecognized transition obligation or $21,450 and 18 percent of the unrecognized prior service cost or $2,970. (2) The gain from the decrease in the accumulated postretirement benefit obligation of $27,000 of $54,000 in excess of the unrecognized net loss of $0 or $27,000. A recognized curtailment gain of $2,580.

(f) Disclosure Requirements.   Like FAS No. 87, "Employers' Accounting For Pension Costs," FAS No. 106 requires extensive disclosures in the notes. The required disclosures provide information not recorded in the accounts or not reported in the financial statements. FAS No. 106 paragraph 74 requires the following disclosures.

1. A description of the substantive plan(s) that is the basis for the accounting, including the nature of the plan, modifications of the existing cost-sharing provisions that are encompassed by the substantive plan(s), the existence and nature of any commitment to increase monetary benefits, employee groups covered, types of benefits provided, funding policy, types of assets held, significant nonbenefit liabilities, and the nature and effect of significant matters affecting the comparability of information for all periods presented, such as the effect of a business combination or divestiture.

2. The amount of net periodic postretirement benefit cost showing separately the service cost component, the interest cost component, the actual return on plan assets for the period, amortization of the unrecognized transition obligation or transition asset, and the net total of other components.

3. A schedule reconciling the funded status of the plan(s) with amounts reported in the employer's statement of financial position.

4. The assumed health care cost trend rate used to measure the expected cost of benefits covered by the plan for the next year and a general description of the direction and pattern of change in the assumed trend rates thereafter, together with the ultimate trend rate and when that rate is expected to be achieved.

5. The weighted-average of the assumed discount rate(s) and rate(s) of compensation increase (for pay related plans) used to measure the accumulated postretirement benefit obligation and the weighted-average of the expected long-term rate(s) of return on plan assets and, for plans whose income is segregated from the employer's investment income for tax purposes, the estimated income tax rate(s) included in that rate of return.

6. The effect of a one-percentage-point increase in the assumed health care cost trend rates for each future year on (a) the aggregate of the service and interest cost components of net periodic postretirement health care benefit cost and (b) the accumulated postretirement benefit obligation for health care benefits.

7. The amounts and types of securities of the employer and related parties included in plan assets, and the approximate amount of future annual benefits of plan participants covered by insurance contracts issued by the employer and related parties.

8. Any alternative amortization method used.

9. The amount of gain or loss recognized during the period for a settlement or curtailment and a description of the nature of the event(s).

CHAPTER 20

DEFERRED TAXES

Ian J. Benjamin
Deloitte & Touche

Frank J. Maurer
United Hospital Medical Center

SUPPLEMENT CONTENTS

20.1 OVERVIEW.

Page 20 · 2, add after SFAS No. 96 in the last paragraph:

and SFAS No. 109

20.2 METHODS OF ACCOUNTING FOR INCOME TAXES.

Page 20 · 6, add at end of first full paragraph:

APB No. 11, however, defined "indefinite" so narrowly that, in U.S. practice, it constituted the comprehensive-allocation-of-income method. In the United Kingdom, SSAP No. 15 allows the preparer of financial statements to look to the foreseeable future rather than the indefinite future, thereby creating a true partial-allocation-of-income method.

20.4 NATIONAL TREATMENTS.

Page 20 · 10, replace the first three paragraphs with:

(i) Current Practice. In February 1992, FASB issued SFAS No. 109 "Accounting for Income Taxes." SFAS 109 is effective for fiscal years beginnning after December 15, 1992. Earlier application is encouraged and some companies have implemented SFAS No. 109 for the year ended December 31, 1991. The new standard employs the comprehensive-allocation method and follows the liability method.

Until SFAS No. 109 is implemented fully, the United States will have three standards any of which might be used by an individual company:

- APB No. 11, the oldest of the three, employs the comprehensive-allocation method and follows the liability method.
- SFAS No. 96, issued in 1987 retains the comprehensive-allocation method but replaces the deferral method with the liability method. The standard was supposed to replace APB No. 11 but concerns were raised that the implementation of SFAS No. 96 was too complex and that the deferred tax asset recognition requirements were too narrow, such that deferred tax assets which are expected to be realized might not be recognized. The effective date for SFAS No. 96 was pushed back repeatedly while these concerns were considered but early application was encouraged and some companies implemented the standard.
- SFAS No. 109 resulted from the reconsideration given to concerns raised as to SFAS No. 96.

Page 20 · 11, add before subsection (ii) Developments:

SFAS No. 109 continued the liability approach of SFAS No. 96, but with a number of changes. SFAS No. 96 requires the detailed scheduling by year of expected reversal for all temporary differences to determine the deferred tax value but precludes consideration of assumptions about future economic events. SFAS No. 109 simplifies the calculation by allowing for the aggregation of temporary differences and one computation of deferred taxes based on applicable tax rates, whereas SFAS No. 96 requires a separate computation to be performed for each year in which the temporary differences reverse. SFAS No. 109 requires the recognition of deferred tax assets, reduced by a valuation allowance if required, for both deductible temporary differences and tax loss or credit carryforwards.

Page 20 · 11, delete the final paragraph of the section.

20.5 SIGNIFICANCE OF VARIATIONS.

Page 20 · 19, insert in Exhibit 20.3 under column Guidance after SFAS No. 96:

and SFAS No. 109

20.6 UNRESOLVED ISSUES.

Page 20 · 21, replace second two sentences in first complete paragraph with:

Three times, in response to preparer criticism, the FASB has had to postpone the implementation of SFAS No. 96 and, finally, replace it with SFAS No. 109.

(c) Treatment of Tax Loss Carryforwards.

Page 20 · 22, add at end of third full paragraph:

* This pattern has been broken to some extent by SFAS No. 109 which requires the recognition of a deferred tax asset for tax loss carryforwards, with a valuation allowance if "based on the weight of evidence, it is *more likely than not* . . . that some portion or all of the deferred tax assets will not be realized" (SFAS No. 109, February 1992). Future experience will tell how conservatively this will be applied.

(d) Location of Deferred Income Taxes in Financial Statements—Liability Section or Shareholders' Equity Section.

Page 20 · 23, insert in Exhibit 20.4 under column Country *after* SFAS No. 96:

and SFAS No. 109

SOURCES AND SUGGESTED REFERENCES

Page 20 · 25, add in alphabetical order:

Financial Accounting Standards Board, Statement of Financial Accounting Standards No. 109, "Accounting for Income Taxes." Stamford, Conn.: FASB, 1992
———. "A Guide to Implementation of Statement 109 on Accounting for Income Taxes—Questions and Answers." Stamford, Conn.: FASB 1992.

Page 20 · 25, replace 1967 *on second line with* 1987.

CHAPTER 21

ACCOUNTING FOR DERIVATIVE PRODUCTS

Fredrick D.S. Choi
New York University

J. Matthew Singleton
Arthur Andersen & Co.

SUPPLEMENT CONTENTS

21.6 INTERNATIONAL PERSPECTIVE.

* *Page 21 • 22, replace Exhibit 21.7 with the following:*

	United States	United Kingdom	Japan	Australia	Germany
1. Direct authoritative guidance	No	Historically, there has been no direct authoritative guidance. There are several exposure drafts outstanding which summarize authoritative viewpoints, for example, The British Bankers Association's ("BBA") draft Statement of Recommended Practice ("SORP") entitled "Commitments and Contingencies."	No	No	No
2. Indirect guidance	FASB No. 80, "Accounting for Futures" FASB No. 52, "Foreign Currency" AICPA issues paper on options EITF Issues 84-7 Termination of swaps 85-36 Interest rate swaps 88-8 Mortgage swaps	The accounting treatment should reflect the underlying economics, subject to complying with accruals and prudence concepts.	Generally influenced by tax policy	Reference is generally made to U.S. practice, or analogy is made to AARB 1012	Nonauthoritative industry-specific pronouncements issued by panels of accounting experts
3. Distinction between dealer and end-user accounting	Yes	Yes	No	Yes	No

4. Dealer accounting	Mark to market	Financial institutions that make a marker or are actively trading in swaps generally mark to market the positions, including adjustments for credit exposure, liquidity, administrative costs, and capital utilization.	Distinction is between banks and other companies. Banks have to mark to market all currency spot, forward, future, and options positions. All other companies' gains and losses are not recorded until final settlement. *Swaps* Net payments and receipts are recognized as adjustments to interest with respect to the asset/liability. Most large companies account for the interest on an accrual basis. All fees are amortized over the life of the swap.	Tendency toward mark to market for speculative transactions- investments are on a cost less permanent diminution basis.	Lower of cost or market

Exhibit 21.7. Accounting for swaps as indicative of treatments for derivatives internationally. This exhibit was prepared with the kind assistance of Eileen Crowley, Arthur Andersen & Co.

	United States	United Kingdom	Japan	Australia	Germany
5. Does hedge accounting exist?	Yes	Yes	*Options* (MOF intends to change the rules). Premiums paid or received should be capitalized and deferred until expiration and sale.	Yes	Yes
6. What risks can be hedged?	Assets and liabilities Macro exposures Firm commitments Anticipated transactions	Assets and liabilities Macro exposures Firm commitments Anticipated transactions	No	Assets and liabilities	Specific assets and liabilities Anticipated transactions
7. What criteria must be met?	Differs by product options, futures, swaps, and F/X See attached chart.	Must eliminate a substantial portion of the risk associated with potential movements in interest rates, exchange rates, and/or market value of the assets, liabilities, or positions being hedged. Transactions must be designated as hedges.	N/A	Differs by product	Binding agreements High correlation of the price development of the instrument and the underlaying Intention to keep the position to maturity

8. Mechanics	Hedge of asset/liability carried at cost. Settlements treated as net adjustments to interest income/expense. Defer and amortize fees all carried at market. Mark to market Recognize fees as incurred Hedge of future transaction Defer and amortize gains, losses, and fees over life of subsequent transaction.	Hedge of asset/liability carried at cost. Fees amortized over the life of the transaction. Income and expenses should be accounted for in the same category of the profit-and-loss account as the income or expense accruing to the asset or liability being hedged. Hedge of asset/liability carried at market. Mark to market	N/A	Settlements treated as net adjustments to interest income/expense:	Settlements treated as net adjustments to interest income/expense.
9. Is practice consistent?	Yes, generally	Yes	Yes	No, except for ASRB 1012	Not always

Exhibit 21.7. (*Continued*)

21.7 SUMMARY.

* *Page 21 · 26, replace second and third complete paragraphs with the following:*

In December 1991, the FASB finalized its second disclosure phase with the issuance of an FASB No. 107 "Disclosures about Fair Value of Financial Instruments" (FASB, 1991). The statement extends existing fair value disclosure practices by requiring all entities to disclose the market value of all financial instruments, both assets and liabilities on and off balance sheet for which it is practicable to estimate market value. Certain types of financial instruments, including lease contracts, deferred compensation arrangements, and insurance contracts, are excluded from the proposed statement's scope. If estimating fair value is not practicable, the following disclosures are called for:

1. Information about the carrying amount, interest rate, maturity, and other characteristics pertinent to estimating the fair value of the financial instrument or class of financial instruments.
2. The reasons why it is not practicable to estimate fair value.

The statement is effective for financial statements issued for fiscal years ending after December 15, 1992. The effective deadline is extended three years for entities whose total assets amount to less than $150 million.

CHAPTER 22

CORPORATE FINANCIAL DISCLOSURE: A GLOBAL ASSESSMENT

Gary K. Meek
Oklahoma State University

David S. Colwell
Coopers & Lybrand

Dennis E. Peavey
Coopers & Lybrand

SUPPLEMENT CONTENTS

22.4 FUNDS OR CASH FLOW STATEMENT.

Page 22 · 9, add after Canada *in the third-from-the-bottom line,* Japan.

Page 22 · 9, replace last sentence with:

With the issuance of FRS No. 1 in 1991, British companies will begin preparing a cash flow statement. FRS No. 1 supercedes SSAP No. 10 which had required a funds statement.

Page 22 · 10, delete second full sentence.

* *Page 22 · 10, replace last sentence with:*

Revised IAS No. 7, "Cash Flow Statements," was issued by the IASC in 1992, calling for the presentation of a cash flow statement (IASC, 1992).

Page 22 · 11, add at the end of the first sentence of the fourth paragraph:

, based on the requirements of SSAP No. 10.

Page 22 · 11, add at the end of the fourth paragraph:

(In September 1991, the U.K. Accounting Standards Board issued FRS No. 1, which supercedes SSAP No. 10.)

Page 22 · 12, replace third sentence of carryover paragraph with:

The U.S. requirement in SFAS No. 95, the new U.K. requirement in FRS No. 1, and the revised IAS No. 7, all reinforce this trend.

Page 22 · 12, delete fourth and fifth sentences of carryover paragraph.

22.7 SHAREHOLDER-ORIENTED INFORMATION.

Page 22 · 19, in the last line on the page, replace most *with* much.

Page 22 · 20, in the first sentence of the carryover paragraph, replace For example, only a few countries *with* However, a number of countries do.

Page 22 · 20, replace last three lines of carryover paragraph with:

excess of a certain percentage of outstanding stock (e.g., France, Japan, United Kingdom, and United States—shareholdings over 5 percent; Canada—shareholdings over 10 percent), and the exchanges where shares are traded (e.g., Japan and United States).

SOURCES AND SUGGESTED REFERENCES

Page 22 · 29, add after third reference:

Accounting Standards Board. Financial Reporting Standard No. 1, "Cash Flow Statements." London: ASB, 1991.

* *Page 22 · 30, add after third reference on this page:*

International Accounting Standards Committee. Revised International Accounting Standard No. 7, "Cash Flow Statements." London: IASC, 1992.

* *Page 22 · 30, delete fourth reference on this page.*

Page 22 · 30, delete fifth reference on this page: "[International Accounting Standards Committee]. Statement of Principles, "Cash Flow Statements." London: IASC, 1990."

CHAPTER **25**

STRATEGIC PLANNING SYSTEMS

Klaus R. Macharzina

Universität Hohenheim, Stuttgart

SUPPLEMENT CONTENTS

25.1 THE STRATEGIC PLANNING ELEMENT IN STRATEGIC MANAGEMENT.

(a) The Strategic Planning Scenario.

* *Page 25 · 1, second paragraph, line 11, replace* U.S.-Canada (plus Mexico) alliance *with the following:*

U.S.-Canada-Mexico alliance (NAFTA),

* *Page 25 · 1 second paragraph, line 13, replace* some . . . U.S.S.R. *with:*

the other member states of the former U.S.S.R.,

25.2 FUNDAMENTALS OF CORPORATE STRATEGIC PLANNING.

(b) Concept of Corporate Strategic Planning.

* *Page 25 · 7, replace* 1991 *with* 1992 *and* 2500 *with* 3000 *in last line of first paragraph.*

CHAPTER 26

MULTINATIONAL BUDGETING AND CONTROL SYSTEMS

Gerald F. Lewis

**Columbia University and
Mobil Corporation**

SUPPLEMENT CONTENTS

26.6 CONTROLLING THE CAPITAL BUDGET.

(c) Status Report Illustration: Current Exchange Rates.

* *Page 26 · 10, replace* PC Variance *column with:*

$$
\begin{array}{r}
400 \\
300 \\
\underline{(200)} \\
\underline{\underline{500}}
\end{array}
$$

26.8 PROFIT PLANNING CONTROLS.

(e) Variance Analysis for Parent Company Use.

* *Page 26 · 20, replace the first Note with:*

The functional currency is the currency of the local company:

CHAPTER 27

FOREIGN INVESTMENT ANALYSIS

David K. Eiteman

**University of California, Los Angeles (Retired) and
Hong Kong University of Science and Technology**

SUPPLEMENT CONTENTS

27.1 General Methodology for One-Country Capital Budgeting.

Page 27 · 4, replace equation in Bottom-Up Approach *with:*

$$
\begin{aligned}
\text{Cash flow} &= \text{NET INCOME } + \text{ DEPRECIATION } + \text{ AMORTIZATION} \\
&\quad + (1\text{-TAX RATE})(\text{INTEREST}) \\
&= 264 + 150 + 50 + (.66)(200) \\
&= 596
\end{aligned}
$$

APPENDIX A

Page 27 · 10, replace Appendix A with:

To illustrate complexities than can arise in the analysis of a foreign investment proposal, a capital budgeting analysis of Penang Chip Company, BhD., a proposed investment in a computer chip manufacturing subsidiary in Penang, Malaysia, is presented. The parent making the investment is Silicon Valley Electronics, Inc., of the United States which will invest the entire equity of MR 52,000,000, or US$18,571,000 at the current exchange rate of MR2.80 = US$1.00. (To avoid confusion, "MR" is used as the symbol for Malaysian ringgits. Within Malaysia the symbol "M$" is normally used.)

If established, Penang Chip will have an initial balance sheet as shown in Exhibit 27.2.
Penang Chip is expected to operate as follows:

1. *Sales:* Physical sales volume will grow at 3% per annum. Initial physical sales volume will be 25,000 units (a unit is a container of chips), and the initial sales price will be MR 5,000 per unit. Initial labor cost is MR 2,000 per unit and initial local material will cost MR 200 per unit. Penang Chip will import material from the United States having an initial cost of $360 per unit. Administrative expenses in the first year will be MR 20 million.

Cash	MR 8,000	Long-term debt	MR 24,000
Accounts receivable	0		
Inventory	8,000		
Net plant & equipment	60,000	Common stock equity	52,000
	MR 76,000		MR 76,000

Note 1: Net plant and equipment will be depreciated on a straight line basis over eight years, with no salvage value.

Note 2: Long-term debt of MR 24,000,000 will be the sole obligation of Penang Chip and will not be guaranteed by Silicon Valley. The regular market interest rate for a Malaysian ringgit debt of this type would be 14%, but Penang Chip is borrowing at a subsidized interest rate of 5% per annum arranged by Malaysian development authorities. The debt will be paid off in five equal annual installments of MR 5,543,000, payable at the end of each year, calculated as follows (rounded to one thousand ringgits):

End of Year	Principal	Interest at 5%	Total Service	Principal Reduction	Remaining Balance
1	24,000	1,200	5,543	4,343	19,657
2	19,657	983	5,543	4,560	15,097
3	15,097	755	5,543	4,788	10,309
4	10,309	515	5,543	5,028	5,281
5	5,281	262	5,543	5,281	-0-

Exhibit 27.2.

2. *Customers:* All production will be sold to unaffiliated buyers in Singapore, Malaysia, and Thailand at sales prices denominated in ringgits.

3. *Malaysian inflation:* Malaysian prices are expected to rise as follow:

Raw material costs:	+ 2% per annum
Labor costs:	+ 5% per annum
General Malaysia prices:	+ 4% per annum
Penang Chip sales prices:	+ 4% per annum

4. *Exchange rate forecasting:* U.S. inflation is expected to be 2% per annum.

Using the theory of purchasing power parity, Silicon Valley expects the ringgit to drop in U.S. dollar value steadily in proportion to the ratio of Malaysian to U.S. inflation, calculated as follows: 1.04/1.02 = 1.0196078, or approximately 1.96% per annum greater inflation in Malaysia. Consequently the exchange rate forecast, by purchasing power parity, is:

Year 0:   MR 2.8000/$
Year 1: MR 2.8000 × 1.0196 = MR 2.8549/$
Year 2: MR 2.8549 × 1.0196 = MR 2.9109/$
Year 3: MR 2.9109 × 1.0196 = MR 2.9680/$
Year 4: MR 2.9680 × 1.0196 = MR 3.0262/$
Year 5: MR 3.0262 × 1.0196 = MR 3.0855/$
Year 6: MR 3.0855 × 1.0196 = MR 3.1460/$

5. **Discount rate**: Silicon Valley has determined that the appropriate discount rate for the Malaysian project is 24% per annum. It will use this rate both within Malaysia (project evaluation) and from its own point of view in the United States (parent evaluation).

6. **Working capital**: Year-end accounts receivable will be equal to 5% of sales of the year just finished. Year-end inventory balances will be maintained at 10% of expected variable costs for the following year. (Additional inventory can be financed with

accounts payable or other current liabilities and so can be ignored for analytical purposes.)

The initial cash balance of MR 8,000,000 will be allowed to increase with retained cash flow in Malaysia. However after operations begin, the cash balance required for operations as of the end of each year will be 6% of expected sales for the following year. Note that this creates what are in effect two cash balances: a "required" cash balance that is a component of working capital, and an "excess" cash balance consisting of funds available for the owners but not removed from the company.

7. **Terminal value**: Silicon Valley expects to sell the subsidiary as a going concern after five years. Although the actual selling price can not be known in advance, Silicon Valley anticipates about an equal probability that the price will be above or below the remaining net book value of fixed assets plus the full value of ending working capital (operating cash, receivables, and inventory); these being the assets necessary for the buyer to continue operations. Cash balances above those needed for operations would not be turned over to the buyer, but would be exchanged for U.S. dollars by Silicon Valley Electronics at the time of sale.

8. **Royalties**: A royalty fee of 5% of sales revenue will be paid by Penang Chip to Silicon Valley each year. This fee creates taxable income in the United States.

9. **Taxes**: Malaysian corporate income taxes are 40%, with no additional dividend withholding tax. The U.S. corporate tax rate is 34%.

10. **Parent exports:** Components imported by Penang Chip from Silicon Valley have a direct manufacturing cost equal to 85% of their transfer price to Penang Chips. Hence Silicon Valley earns a dollar profit and cash flow, before United States income taxes, equal to 15% of all sales to Penang Chip. Malaysian production and sales will not cause any loss of sales from any other Silicon Valley plant elsewhere in the world.

11. **Dividends**: Silicon Valley intends to have Penang Chip declare 75% of its accounting profit as dividends each year. Malaysian authorities have indicated, informally, that this is appropriate.

Penang Chip's pro forma income statement for the first year of operations is shown as column 1 of Exhibit 27.3. The remainder of Exhibit 27.3 shows expected income accounts over the following five years in accordance with the expectations and guidelines described above.

Components of Valuation:

Exhibit 27.3 shows a growing annual revenue, matched by increased costs. Line 17 indicates that the project is profitable in every year, and line 18 shows the expected cash dividend to Silicon Valley,

Exhibit 27.4 shows the annual increase in investment in the operating cash balance, accounts receivable, and inventory, as well as in free cash balances. Note that receivables levels are based on sales of the past year, while inventory levels depend on expected sales for the following year, which means that variable costs for the sixth year must be calculated to determine inventory required at the end of the fifth year. Total cash balance has two components: an operating balance required for daily needs and hence not available to owners unless the business is liquidated, and a free cash balance available for discretionary purposes at any time.

Exhibit 27.5 shows the current asset balances after five years of operations—balances which are necessary to calculate the terminal value.

Exhibit 27.6 shows how terminal value is estimated for the end of five years. In this instances, expected terminal value has been specified to be equal to the ending net book value of plant and equipment, plus ending current assets. Obviously a terminal value many years in the future is subjective, and other methods of estimating this future value are possible. In this instance, Silicon Valley Electronics expects to receive MR 52,964,000 for Penang Chip after

PENANG CHIP
Revenue, Expenses, and Profit for Years 1 Through 5
(In Thousands of Malaysian Ringgits, Except for Unit Costs)

	1	2	3	4	5
Revenue					
1. Unit volume (g = 3%)	25,000	25,750	26,522	27,318	28,138
2. Unit price (g = 4%)	5,000	5,200	5,408	5,624	5,849
3. Total sales revenue	125,000	133,900	143,431	153,636	164,579
Unit Variable Costs					
4. Local labor (g = 5%)	2,000	2,100	2,205	2,315	2,431
5. Local material (g = 2%)	200	204	208	212	216
6. U.S. parent (note 1)	1,028	1,068	1,113	1,156	1,203
7. Variable cost/unit	3,228	3,372	3,526	3,683	3,850
8. Total varib. costs	80,700	86,829	93,517	100,612	108,331
Cost and Profit Data					
9. Gross profit (3-9)	44,300	47,071	49,914	53,024	56,248
10. Royalaties (5% × Sales)	6,250	6,695	7,172	7,682	8,229
11. Administration (g = 4%)	20,000	20,800	21,632	22,497	23,397
12. Depreciation	7,500	7,500	7,500	7,500	7,500
13. Earnings Before Interest and Taxes (EBIT)	10,550	12,076	13,610	15,375	17,122
14. Interest expense	1,200	983	755	515	262
15. Pretax income	9,350	11,093	12,855	14,860	16,860
16. 40% Malaysian tax	−3,740	−4,437	−5,142	−5,944	−6,744
17. Net income	5,610	6,656	7,713	8,916	10,116
18. Cash dividends @75%	4,207	4,992	5,785	6,687	7,587

Note 1: U.S. raw material supplied will rise in dollar price at 2% per annum with U.S. inflation. The ringgit equivalent on a per unit basis is calculated as follows. The sixth year calculation is necesary for forecasting fifth year inventory.

	1	2	3	4	5	6
Unit sales price in $ (g = 2%)	$360	$367	$375	$382	$390	$397
Exchange rate	2.8549	2.9109	2.9680	3.0262	3.0855	3.1460
Ringgit unit cost	1,028	1,068	1,113	1,156	1,203	1,249

Exhibit 27.3.

PENANG CHIP
Working Capital and Free Cash Accumulation
(In Thousands of Malaysian Ringgits)

	1	2	3	4	5
Operating Cash Balance					
1. Sales revenue	125,000	133,900	143,431	153,636	164,579
2. Required cash, @ 6% of following years' sales[a]	8,034	8,605	9,218	9,875	10,578
3. Increase over prior balance	34	571	613	657	703
Accounts Receivable					
4. Sales revenue	125,000	133,900	143,431	153,636	164,579
5. Required A/R, @ 5% of current sales	6,250	6,695	7,172	7,682	8,229
6. Increase over prior balance	6,250	445	477	510	547
Inventory					
7. Varib. costs	80,700	86,829	93,517	100,612	108,331
8. Required inventory @ 10% of next year's variable costs[b]	8,683	9,352	10,061	10,833	11,657
9. Increase over prior year's balance	683	669	709	772	824
Free Cash Balances[c]					
10. Net income (Exhibit 27.3, line 17)	5,610	6,656	7,713	8,916	10,116
11. Less 75% dividends	−4,207	−4,992	−5,785	−6,687	−7,587
12. Earnings retained (25% of net income)	1,403	1,664	1,928	2,229	2,529
13. Plus depreciation	+7,500	+7,500	+7,500	+7,500	+7,500
14. Less increase in operating cash balance (line 3 above)	−34	−571	−613	−657	−703
15. Less increase in accounts receivable (line 6 above)	−6,250	−445	−477	−510	−547
16. Less increase in inventory (line 9 above)	−683	−669	−709	−772	−824
17. Addition to free cash balance from operations	1,936	7,479	7,629	7,790	7,955
18. Less repayment of debt principal (Exhibit 27.2, note 2)	−4,343	−4,560	−4,788	−5,028	−5,281
19. Annual addition to free cash balance	−2,407	2,919	2,841	2,762	2,674

[a] Projected 6th year sales are (MR 164,579,000) (1.03) (1.04) = MR 176,296,000. Required cash at the end of the fifth year equals (6%) (MR 176,296,000) = MR 10,577,760. "Operating cash" is a mandatory component of working capital.

[b] Variable costs in the sixth year are calculated as follows:

Sixth year labor.	(1.05) (2,431) =	$2,553
Sixth year local material.	(1.02) (216) =	220
Sixth year U.S. material, from Note 1, Ex 2		1,249
Total unit variable costs		$4,022
Times volume (1.03) (28,138)		×28,982
Total sixth year variable costs		$116,566

[c] For valuation purposes, total cash balance is divided into two segments: operating cash balance and free cash balance. Operating cash balance is a working capital component necessary for operations, and is "recovered" only at the time a terminal value is received. Free cash balance is available for discretionary purposes at any time, and increments to free cash balance have been valued in the year of receipt. Hence from a project point of view, they can not also be valued a second time as a component of terminal value. From a parent point of view, they are valued when received in the United States.

Exhibit 27.4.

PENANG CHIP
Current Asset Balances after Five Years
(In Thousands of Malaysian Ringgits)

	Operating Cash	A/R	Inventory	Free Cash
1. Initial balance	8,000	0	8,000	0
2. Year 1 addition	34	6,250	683	−2,407
3. Year 2 addition	571	445	669	2,919
4. Year 3 addition	613	477	709	2,841
5. Year 4 addition	657	510	772	2,762
6. Year 5 addition	703	547	824	2,674
7. Ending balances	10,578	8,229	11,657	8,789

Note 1: Initial operating cash balance, a component of required working capital, is from Exhibit 27.2. Additions to operating cash balances are from line 3 of Exhibit 27.4. Additions to receivables and inventory balances are from lines 6 and 9 of Exhibit 27.4. Additions to free cash balances are from line 19 of Exhibit 27.4.

Exhibit 27.5.

five years. Because this amount consists entirely of the recovery of original outlays (i.e., no capital gains), it would be received free of any income taxes.

The present value of the subsidized loan is calculated in Exhibit 27.7. The essence of the calculation is that the net after-tax repayments at a 5% subsidized rate are subtracted from the net after-tax payments at a 14% market rate of interest. The difference is the annual value of the subsidy, and the value of the subsidized loan is equal to the present value of these individual values. The net present value of the subsidy is shown to be MR 2,841,000.

Project Valuation:

Exhibit 27.8 shows that the present value of operating inflows, calculated on an all-equity basis, is MR 50,978,000. To this must be added the net present value of the subsidized loan, which is MR 2,841,000. Subtracting the original outlay of MR 76,000,000 leaves a **negative** net present value of MR 22,181,000. This that means that from the point of view of the project, the investment is not worth undertaking: its cost in today's ringgits is greater than the present value of all expected future cash receipts.

The fact that Penang Chip has a negative net present value as a project means that investors would not find it worth while as a stand-alone operation within Malaysia. This negative net present value as a project, however, is separate from the value of the project to its parent, Silicon Valley.

PENANG CHIP
Terminal Value at the End of Five Years

1. Original cost of net plant and equipment	MR 60,000,000
2. Less depreciation for five years @ MR 7,500,000/yr	−37,500,000
3. Net book value of plant & equipment	MR 22,500,000
4. Plus ending operating cash balance (Exhibit 27.5, line 7)	+10,578,000
5. Plus ending receivable balance (Exhibit 27.5, line 7)	+8,229,000
6. Plus ending inventory (Exhibit 27.5, line 7)	+11,657,000
7. Terminal value in year 5	MR 52,964,000

Exhibit 27.6.

PENANG CHIP
Present Value of Subsidized Loan
(In Thousands of Malaysian Ringgits)

Payments on the 5% subsidized loan appear in Note 2 to Exhibit 27.2. Payments on a 14% loan would be MR 6,990,000 per year, as follows:

End of Year	Principal	Interest at 14%	Total Service	Principal Reduction	Remaining Balance
1	24,000	3,360	6,990	3,630	20,370
2	20,370	2,852	6,990	4,138	16,231
3	16,231	2,272	6,990	4,718	11,513
4	11,513	1,612	6,990	5,378	6,135
5	6,135	859	6,990	6,131	0

	0	1	2	3	4	5
14% loan (at market):						
1. Principal	+24,000					
2. Loan: principal repayments:		−3,630	−4,138	−4,718	−5,378	−6,131
3. Loan: interest payment		−3,360	−2,852	−2,272	−1,612	−859
4. Tax saving at 40% of interest		+1,344	+1,140	+909	+645	+344
5. Net after-tax cash repayments		−5,646	−5,850	−6,081	−6,345	−6,646
5% loan (subsidized):						
6. Principal	+24,000					
7. Loan: principal repayments:		−4,343	−4,560	−4,788	−5,028	−5,281
8. Loan: interest payment		−1,200	−983	−755	−515	−262
9. Tax saving at 40% of interest		+480	+393	+302	+206	+105
10. Net after-tax cash repayments		−5,063	−5,150	−5,241	−5,337	−5,438
Difference:						
11. Advantage of subsidized loan (line 5–line 10)	0	583	700	840	1,008	1,208
12. PV factor @ 14%	1.0000	.8772	.7695	.6750	.5921	.5194
13. Annual PV of advantage	0	511	539	567	597	627
14. Net PV of advantage	+2,841					

Exhibit 27.7.

PENANG CHIP
Project Net Present Value, All-Equity Basis
(In Thousands of Malaysian Ringgits)

	1	2	3	4	5
1. EBIT: Earnings before interest and taxes (Exhibit 27.3, line 13)	10,550	12,076	13,610	15,375	17,122
2. Less 40% income taxes (note 1)	−4,220	−4,830	−5,444	−6,150	−6,849
3. All-equity net income	6,330	7,246	8,166	9,225	10,273
4. Plus depreciation	+7,500	+7,500	+7,500	+7,500	+7,500
5. Less increase in mandatory cash (Exhibit 27.4, line 3)	−34	−571	−613	−657	−703
6. Less increase in receivable balance (Exhibit 27.4, line 6)	−6,250	−445	−477	−510	−547
7. Less increase in inventory balance (Exhibit 27.4, line 9)	−683	−669	−709	−772	−824
8. Plus terminal value (Exhibit 27.6, line 6)					52,964
9. Net project cash flow	6,863	13,061	13,867	14,786	68,633
10. 24% PV factor	.8065	.6504	.5245	.4230	.3411
11. Present value of each annual free cash inflow	5,535	8,495	7,273	6,254	23,421

	Year 0
12. Sum of present value of annual free cash inflows	+50,978
13. Present value of subsidized loan (Exhibit 27.7, line 14)	+2,841
14. Original outflow (Exhibit 27.2)	−76,000
15. Net present value	−22,181

Note 1: Malaysian income taxes shown on line 2 are not actual taxes paid, but are rather the taxes that would have been paid had Penang Chip been financed entirely with equity. Only actual taxes paid, rather than hypothetical taxes based on an all-equity assumption, are allowable as a credit against U.S. taxes on dividends received.

Exhibit 27.8.

Parent Valuation:

The value of Penang Chip to its U.S. parent is calculated in Exhibit 27.9 to be a **positive** US$305,000. Several reasons exist why this value is different both in amount and, in this instance, in sign, from value as a project. Basically the reasons are because the cash flows in the respective cases differ. The major differences are:

1. *Total cash flow versus dividends:* From a project point-of-view, all cash generated contributes to value because it is available within Malaysia. From a parent point of view, cash has no value until received Silicon Valley in the United States. I.e., retained earnings and

PENANG CHIP
Net Present Value to Silicon Valley—Parent Perspective
(In Thousands of Malaysian Ringgits and U.S. Dollars)

	1	2	3	4	5
In Ringgits					
1. Malaysian royalties					
(Exhibit 27.3, line 10)	6,250	6,695	7,172	7,682	8,229
2. U.S. tax @ 34%	−2,125	−2,276	−2,438	−2,612	−2,798
3. Net royalty	4,125	4,419	4,734	5,070	5,431
4. Malaysian dividend					
(Exhibit 27.3, line 18)	4,207	4,992	5,785	6,687	7,587
5. Terminal value					
(Exhibit 27.6, line 6)					52,964
6. Free cash flow recovered					
(Exhibit 27.5, line 7)					8,789
7. Total cash flow to parent	8,332	9,411	10,519	11,757	74,771
8. Forecast exchange rate	2.8549	2.9109	2.9680	3.0262	3.0855
In Dollars					
9. Cash flow from Malaysia	2,918	3,233	3,544	3,885	24,233
10. Export contribution					
(note 1)	891	936	985	1,033	1,086
11. Total dollar inflow	3,809	4,169	4,529	4,918	25,319
12. 24% PV factor	.8065	.6504	.5245	.4230	.3411
13. Present value of inflows	3,072	2,712	2,376	2,080	8,636

Year 0

14. Sum of present value of inflows	+18,876
15. Less original outflow	−18,571
16. Net present value	+305

Note 1: Silicon Valley's U.S. dollar profit (15% of sales) on exports to Malaysia is as follows:

	1	2	3	4	5
Unit sales price in					
$ (g = 2%)	$ 360	$ 367	$ 375	$ 382	$ 390
Unit volume	25,000	25,750	26,522	27,318	28,138
Dollar revenue	$ 9,000	$ 9,450	$ 9,946	$10,435	$10,974
Contribution to pre-tax					
profit (15%)	1,350	1,418	1,492	1,565	1,646
U.S. 34% tax	−459	−482	−507	−532	−560
Net cash contribution to					
parent	$ 891	$ 936	$ 985	$ 1,033	$ 1,086

Exhibit 27.9.

funds equal to depreciation charges are valued at once in the host country, but only when and if recovered (or completely available to be recovered) by the parent country.

2. *Free cash flow:* Free cash flow (cash flow greater than needed for day-to-day operations) is valued at the time received in the project approach, but only when remitted to the parent company as a liquidating dividend from a parent point of view.

3. *Royalties:* Royalties and similar charges paid by Penang to Silicon Valley are not part of cash flow in the project valuation (they are an outflow), but are an important portion of the value to Silicon Valley. This suggests that if the parent exports sufficient items of value to its foreign subsidiary, the project may be worthwhile to the parent even though it fails to pass the project net-present value criteria.

4. *Subsidized loan:* The present value of the subsidized loan does not show as a cash flow to the parent because the loan is reflected in increased cash retention by the subsidiary over the five years. Silicon Valley benefits only from the higher terminal value and free cash recovered.

5. *Taxes:* In many instances, different income tax treatment of cash flows may influence one or the other valuation approaches.

Regardless of whether the proposal has a positive or negative net present value as a project from the parent perspective, the capital budgeting approach provides insight into techniques management might use to increase the value of the firm. Basically, management should seek ways to reduce investment outlay (perhaps subcontracting part of projection), increase revenue (perhaps raising sales prices in or some market if this can be done without a loss of volume), or reduce operating costs (perhaps using a different degree of technology or automation to reduce costs) so as to generate more positive net present value. Another possibility would be to increase the transfer price on components sold by Silicon Valley to Penang Chip. All such steps will have cash flow consequences for both Silicon Value and Penang Chip. However a finance manager should be a "doer" rather than only a passive analyzer of data collected from others, so such a manager should participate in the search for any combination of cash flows that will increase the positive net present value.

In some instances management may decide to proceed with a project even if parent net present value is negative. Usually this is for reasons of global strategy, although the idea may be expressed in financial terms as acknowledgement that some long-run global advantages can be achieved which can not be quantified in estimated cash flows. Some will argue that this introduction of non-quantified subjectivity destroys the rigor of the net present value to capital budgeting, while others will argue that recognition of long-run non-quantifiable strategic goals is an important part of management's judgment and hence is vital to success.

Last, parent net present value may be influenced by how the project interacts with other international ventures. Under present U.S. tax law (which could be changed), dividends from operations in countries where the income tax rate is above the U.S. tax rate generate "excess" (i.e., lost) tax credits. These excess tax credits can be used only if dividends of a similar nature are declared from other subsidiaries operating in jurisdictions where the tax rate is below the U.S. tax rate, so that the high taxes of one foreign jurisdiction can be combined with the low taxes of another foreign jurisdiction to minimize overall total U.S. taxes levied on the total post-tax dividends received from all foreign countries.*

---

* For a detailed explanation of this pooling of tax credits, see pages 644–646 of David K. Eiteman, Arthur I. Stonehill, and Michael H. Moffett, *Multinational Business Finance,* 6th ed. Reading, Massachusetts: Addison-Wesley Publishing Company, 1992.

CHAPTER **27A**

THE MANAGEMENT OF FOREIGN EXCHANGE RISK (NEW)

Ian H. Giddy
New York University

Gunter Dufey
University of Michigan

SUPPLEMENT CONTENTS

27A.1 GOALS OF THE CHAPTER. Exchange risk is the effect that unanticipated exchange rate changes have on the value of the firm. This chapter explores the impact of currency fluctuations on cash flows, on assets and liabilities, and on the real business of the firm. Three questions must be asked: (1) What exchange risk does the firm face, and what methods are available to measure currency exposure? (2) Based on the nature of the exposure and the firm's ability to forecast currencies, what hedging or exchange risk management strategy should the firm employ? (3) Which of the various tools and techniques of the foreign exchange market should be employed: debt and assets; forwards and futures; and options. The chapter concludes by suggesting a framework that can be used to match the instrument to the problem.

Exchange risk is simple in concept: a potential gain or loss that occurs as a result of an exchange rate change. For example, if an individual owns a share in Hitachi, a Japanese company, he or she will lose if the value of the yen drops.

Yet from this simple concept several questions arise. First, whose gain or loss—Not just those of a subsidiary, for they may be offset by positions taken elsewhere in the firm. And not just gains or losses on current transactions, for the firm's value consist of anticipated future cash flows as well as currently contracted ones. What counts is shareholder value; yet the impact of any given currency change on shareholder value is difficult to assess, so proxies have to be used. The academic evidence linking exchange rate changes to stock prices is weak.

Moreover, the shareholder who has a diversified portfolio may find that the negative effect of exchange rate changes on one firm is offset by gains in other firms; in other words, that exchange risk is diversifiable. If it is, than perhaps it's a nonrisk.

Finally, risk is not risk if it is anticipated. In most currencies, there are futures or forward exchange contracts whose prices give firms an indication of where the market expects currencies to go. And these contracts offer the ability to lock in the anticipated change. So perhaps a better concept of exchange risk is *unanticipated* exchange rate changes.

These and other issues justify a closer look at this area of international financial management.

27A.2 SHOULD FIRMS MANAGE FOREIGN EXCHANGE RISK?   Many firms refrain from active management of their foreign exchange exposure, even though they understand that exchange rate fluctuations can affect their earnings and value. They make this decision for a number of reasons.

First, management does not understand it. They consider any use of risk management tools, such as forwards, futures and options, as speculative. Or they argue that such financial manipulations lie outside the firm's field of expertise. "We are in the business of manufacturing slot machines, and we should not be gambling on currencies." Perhaps they are right to fear abuses of hedging techniques, but refusing to use forwards and other instruments may expose the firm to substantial speculative risks.

Second, they claim that exposure cannot be measured. They are right—currency exposure is complex and can seldom be gauged with precision. But as in many business situations, imprecision should not be taken as an excuse for indecision.

Third, they say that the firm *is* hedged. All transactions such as imports or exports are covered, and foreign subsidiaries finance in local currencies. This ignores the fact that the bulk of the firm's value comes from transactions not yet completed, so that transactions hedging is a very incomplete strategy.

Fourth, they say that the firm does not have any exchange risk because it does all its business in dollars (or yen, or whatever the home currency is). But a moment's thought will make it evident that even if you invoice German customers in dollars, when the mark drops your prices will have to adjust or you'll be undercut by local competitors. So revenues are influenced by currency changes.

Finally, they assert that the balance sheet is hedged on an accounting basis—especially when the "functional currency" is held to be the dollar. The misleading signals that balance sheet exposure measure can give are documented in later sections. But is there any *economic* justification for a "do nothing" strategy?

Modern principles of the theory of finance suggest *prima facie* that the management of corporate foreign exchange exposure may neither be an important nor a legitimate concern. It has been argued, in the tradition of the Modigliani-Miller Theorem, that the firm cannot improve shareholder value by financial manipulations; specifically, investors themselves can hedge corporate exchange exposure by taking out forward contracts in accordance with their ownership in a firm. Managers do not serve them by second guessing what risks shareholders want to hedge.

One counterargument is that transaction costs are typically greater for individual investors than firms. Yet there are deeper reasons why foreign exchange risk should be managed at the firm level. As will be shown, the assessment of exposure to exchange rate fluctuations requires detailed estimates of the susceptibility of net cash flows to unexpected exchange rate changes

(Dufey and Srinivasulu, 1983). Operating managers can make such estimates with much more precision than shareholders who typically lack the detailed knowledge of competition, markets, and the relevant technologies. Furthermore, in all but the most perfect financial markets, the firm has considerable advantages over investors in obtaining relatively inexpensive debt at home and abroad, taking maximum advantage of interest subsidies and minimizing the effect of taxes and political risk.

Another line of reasoning suggests that foreign exchange risk management does not matter because of certain equilibrium conditions in international markets for both financial and real assets. These conditions include the relationship between prices of goods in different markets, better known as Purchasing Power Parity (PPP), and between interest rates and exchange rates, usually referred to as the International Fisher Effect (Section 27A.3).

However, deviations from PPP and IFE can persist for considerable periods of time, especially at the level of the individual firm. The resulting variability of net cashflow is of significance as it can subject the firm to the costs of *financial distress,* or even default. Modern research in finance supports the reasoning that earnings fluctuations that threaten the firm's continued viability absorb management and creditor's time, entail out-of-pocket costs such as legal fees, and create a variety of operating and investment problems, including underinvestment in R&D. The same argument supports the importance of corporate exchange risk management against the claim that in equity markets it is only systematic risk that matters. To the extent that foreign exchange risk represents unsystematic risk, it can, of course, be diversified away—provided again, that investors have the same quality of information about the firm as management—a condition not likely to prevail in practice.

This reasoning is buttressed by the likely effect that exchange risk has on *taxes* paid by the firm. It is generally agreed that leverage shields the firm from taxes, because interest is tax deductible whereas dividends are not. But the extent to which a firm can increase leverage is limited by the risk and costs of bankruptcy. It follows that anything that reduces the probability of bankruptcy allows the firm to take on greater leverage, and so pay less taxes for a given operating cash flow. If foreign exchange hedging reduces taxes, shareholders benefit from hedging.

However, there is one task that the firm cannot perform for shareholders: to the extent that individuals face unique exchange risk as a result of their different expenditure patterns, they must themselves devise appropriate hedging strategies. Corporate management of foreign exchange risk in the traditional sense is only able to protect expected *nominal* returns in the reference currency (Eaker, 1981).

27A.3 ECONOMIC EXPOSURE, PURCHASING POWER PARITY, AND THE INTERNATIONAL FISHER EFFECT.   Exchange rates, interest rates, and inflation rates are linked to one another through a classical set of relationships which have import for the nature of corporate foreign exchange risk. These relationships are: (1) the *purchasing power parity* theory, which describes the linkage between relative inflation rates and exchanges rates; (2) the *international Fisher effect,* which ties interest rate differences to exchange rate expectations; and (3) the *unbiased forward rate theory,* which relates the forward exchange rate to exchange rate expectations. These relationships, along with two other key "parity" linkages, are illustrated in Figure 27A.1.

The *Purchasing Power Parity* (PPP) theory can be stated in different ways, but the most common representation links the changes in exchange rates to those in relative price indices in two countries.

Rate of change of exchange rate = Difference in inflation rates

The relationship is derived from the basic idea that, in the absence of trade restrictions changes in the exchange rate mirror changes in the relative price levels in the two countries. At the same time, under conditions of free trade, prices of similar commodities cannot differ between two countries, because arbitragers will take advantage of such situations until price differences are

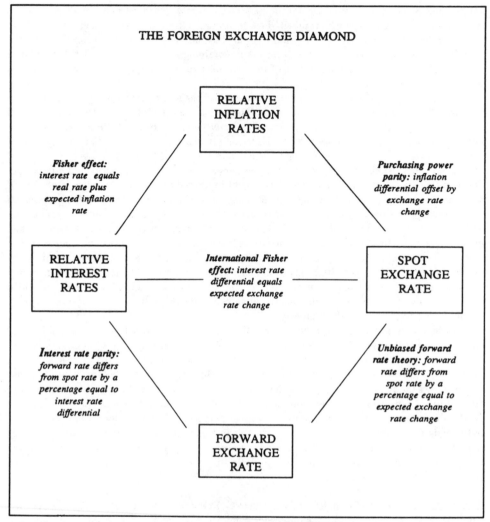

Exhibit 27A.1.   Key parity relationships of international finance that affect corporate exchange risk exposure.

eliminated. This *Law of One Price* leads logically to the idea that what is true of one commodity should be true of the economy as a whole—the price level in two countries should be linked through the exchange rate—and hence to the notion that exchange rate changes are tied to inflation rate differences.

The *International Fisher Effect* (IFE) states that the interest rate differential will exist only if the exchange rate is expected to change in such a way that the advantage of the higher interest rate is offset by the loss on the foreign exchange transactions.

This International Fisher Effect can be written as follows:

The expected rate of change of the exchange rate = The interest rate differential

In practical terms, the IFE implies that while an investor in a low-interest country can convert his funds into the currency of the high-interest country and get paid a higher rate, his gain (the interest rate differential) will be offset by his expected loss because of foreign exchange rate changes.

The *Unbiased Forward Rate Theory* asserts that the forward exchange rate is the best, and an unbiased, estimate of the expected future spot exchange rate. The theory is grounded in the efficient markets theory, and is widely assumed and widely disputed as a precise explanation.

The "expected rate" is only an average but the theory of efficient markets tell us that it is an *unbiased* expectation—that there is an equal probability of the actual rate being above or below the expected value.

The unbiased forward rate theory can be stated:

$$\text{The expected exchange rate} = \text{The forward exchange rate}$$

Now we can summarize the impact of unexpected exchange rate changes on the internationally involved firm by drawing on these parity conditions. Given sufficient time, competitive forces and arbitrage will neutralize the impact of exchange rate changes on the returns to assets; due to the relationship between rates of devaluation and inflation differentials, these factors will also neutralize the impact of the changes on the value of the firm. This is the principle of Purchasing Power Parity and the Law of One Price operating at the level of the firm. On the liability side, the cost of debt tends to adjust as debt is repriced at the end of the contractual period, reflecting (revised) expected exchange rate changes. And returns on equity will also reflect required rates of return; in a competitive market these will be influenced by expected exchange rate changes. Finally, the unbiased forward rate theory suggests that locking in the forward exchange rate offers the same expected return as remaining exposed to the ups and downs of the currency—on average, it can be expected to err as much above as below the forward rate.

In the long run, it would seem that a firm operating in this setting will not experience net exchange losses or gains. However, because of contractual, or, more importantly, strategic commitments, these equilibrium conditions rarely hold in the short and medium term. Therefore the essence of foreign exchange exposure, and, significantly, its management, are made relevant by these "temporary deviations."

27A.4 IDENTIFYING EXPOSURE.   The first step in management of corporate foreign exchange risk is to acknowledge that such risk does exist and that managing it is in the interest of the firm and its shareholders. The next step, however, is much more difficult: the identification of the nature and magnitude of foreign exchange exposure. In other words, identifying what is at risk, and in what way.

The focus here is on the exposure of (nonfinancial) corporations, or rather the value of their assets. This reminder is necessary because most commonly accepted notions of foreign exchange risk hedging deal with *financial* assets, that is, they are pertinent to (simple) financial institutions where the bulk of the assets consists of (paper) assets that have with contractually fixed returns, such as, fixed income claims, not equities. Such time-honored hedging rules as "finance your assets in the currency in which they are denominated" applies in general to banks and similar firms. Nonfinancial business firms, on the other hand, have only a relatively small proportion of their total assets in the form of receivables and other financial claims. Their core assets consist of inventories, equipment, special purpose buildings and other tangible assets, often closely related to technological capabilities that give them earnings power and thus value. Unfortunately, real assets (as compared to paper assets) are not labelled with currency signs that make foreign exchange exposure analysis easy. Most importantly, the location of an asset in a country is—as we shall see—an all too fallible indicator of their foreign exchange exposure.

The task of gauging the impact of exchange rate changes on an enterprise begins with measuring its *exposure,* that is, the amount, or value, at risk. This issue has been clouded by the fact that financial results for an enterprise tend to be compiled by methods based on the principles of accrual accounting. Unfortunately, this approach yields data that frequently differ from those relevant for business decision-making, namely future cashflows and their associated risk profiles. As a result, considerable efforts are expended—both by decision makers as well as students of exchange risk—to reconcile the differences between the point-in-time effects of exchange rate changes on an enterprise in terms of accounting data, referred to as *accounting* or *translation exposure,* and the ongoing cash flow effects which are referred to as *economic exposure.* Both concepts have their grounding in the fundamental concept of *transactions exposure.* The relationship between the three concepts is illustrated in Exhibit 27A.2. While exposure concepts have been aptly analyzed elsewhere in this *Handbook* (Chapter 15 by Professor Trevor Harris), some basic concepts are repeated here.

(a) Exposure in a Simple Transaction.   The typical illustration of transaction exposure involves an export or import contract giving rise to a foreign currency receivable or payable. On the surface, when the exchange rate changes, the value of this export or import transaction will be affected in terms of the domestic currency. However, when analyzed carefully, it becomes apparent that the exchange risk results from a financial investment (the foreign currency receivable) or a foreign currency liability (the loan from a supplier) that is purely incidental to the underlying export or import transaction; it could have arisen in and of itself through independent foreign borrowing and lending. Thus, what is involved here are simply foreign currency assets and liabilities, whose denominal value is contractually fixed in nominal terms.

While this traditional analysis of transactions exposure is correct in a narrow, formal sense, it is really relevant for financial institutions, only. With returns from financial assets and liabilities being fixed in nominal terms, they can be shielded from losses with relative ease through cash payments in advance (with appropriate discounts), through the factoring of receivables, or via the use of forward exchange contracts, unless unexpected exchange rate changes have a systematic effect on credit risk. However, the essential assets of nonfinancial firms have *noncontractual* returns, that is, revenue and cost streams from the production and sale of their goods and services which can respond to exchange rate changes in very different

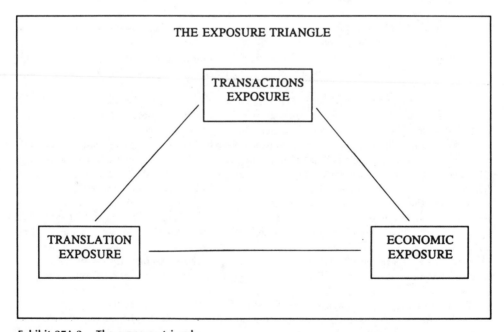

Exhibit 27A.2.   The exposure triangle.

ways. Consequently, they are characterized by foreign exchange exposure very different from that of firms with contractual returns.

(b) Accounting Exposure.   The concept of accounting exposure arises from the need to translate accounts that are denominated in foreign currencies into the home currency of the reporting entity. Most commonly the problem arises when an enterprise has foreign affiliates keeping books in the respective local currency. For purposes of consolidation, these accounts must somehow be *translated* into the reporting currency of the parent company. In doing this, a decision must be made as to the exchange rate that is to be used for the translation of the various accounts. While income statements of foreign affiliates are typically translated at a periodic *average* rate, balance sheets pose a more serious challenge.

To a certain extent this difficulty is revealed by the struggle of the accounting profession to agree on appropriate translation rules and the treatment of the resulting gains and losses. A comparative historical analysis of translation rules may best illustrate the issues at hand. Over time, U.S. companies have followed essentially four types of translation methods, summarized in Exhibit 27A.3. These four methods differ with respect to the presumed impact of exchange rate changes on the value of individual categories of assets and liabilities. Accordingly, each method can be identified by the way in which it separates assets and liabilities into those that are "exposed" and are, therefore, translated at the current rate, that is, the rate prevailing on the date of the balance sheet, and those whose value is deemed to remain unchanged, and which are, therefore, translated at the historical rate.

The *current/noncurrent* method of translation divides assets and liabilities into current and noncurrent categories, using maturity as the distinguishing criterion; only the former are presumed to change in value when the local currency appreciates or depreciates vis-à-vis the home currency. Supporting this method is the economic rationale that foreign exchange rates are essentially fixed but subject to occasional adjustments that tend to correct themselves in time.

	Current/ Noncurrent	Monetary/ Nonmonetary	Temporal	Current
ASSETS				
Cash	C	C	C	C
Marketable Securities (At Market Value)	C	C	C	C
Accounts Receivable	C	C	C	C
Inventory (At Cost)	C	H	H	C
Fixed Assets	H	H	H	C
LIABILITIES				
Current Liablities	C	C	C	C
Long Term Debt	H	C	C	C
Equity	Residual Adjustment	Residual Adjustment	Residual Adjustment	Residual Adjustment

Note: In the case of Income Statements, sales revenues and interest are generally translated at the average historical exchange rate that prevailed during the period; depreciation is translated at the appropriate historical exchange rate. Some of the general and administrative expenses as well as cost-of-goods-sold are translated at historical exchange rates, others at current rates.

"C" = Assets and liabilities are translated at the current rate, or rate prevailing on the date of the balance sheet.

"H" = Assets and liabilities are translated at the historical rate.

Exhibit 27A.3.   Methods of translation for balance sheets.

This assumption reflected reality to some extent, particularly with respect to industrialized countries during the period of the Bretton Woods system. However, with subsequent changes in the international financial environment, this translation method has become outmoded; only in a few countries is it still being used.

Under the *monetary/nonmonetary* method all items explicitly defined in terms of monetary units are translated at the current exchange rate, regardless of their maturity. Nonmonetary items in the balance sheet, such as tangible assets, are translated at the historical exchange rate. The underlying assumption here is that the local currency value of such assets increases (decreases) immediately after a devaluation (revaluation) to a degree that compensates fully for the exchange rate change. This is equivalent of what is known in economics as the *Law of One Price,* with instantaneous adjustments.

A similar but more sophisticated translation approach supports the so-called *temporal* method. Here, the exchange rate used to translate balance sheet items depends on the valuation method used for a particular item in the balance sheet. Thus, if an item is carried on the balance sheet of the affiliate at its current value, it is to be translated using the current exchange rate. Alternatively, items carried at historical cost are to be translated at the historical exchange rate. As a result, this method synchronizes the time dimension of valuation with the method of translation. As long as foreign affiliates compile balance sheets under traditional historical cost principles, the temporal method gives essentially the same results as the monetary/nonmonetary method. However, when "current value accounting" is used, that is, when accounts are adjusted for inflation, then the temporal method calls for the use of the current exchange rate throughout the balance sheet.

The temporal method provided the conceptual base for the Financial Accounting Standard Board's Standard 8 (FAS 8), which came into effect in 1976 for all U.S.-based companies and those non-U.S. companies that had to follow U.S. accounting principles in order to raise funds in the public markets of the United States.

The temporal method points to a more general issue: the relationship between translation and valuation methods for accounting purposes. When methods of valuation provide results that do not reflect economic reality, translation will fail to remedy that deficiency, but will tend to make the distortion very apparent. To illustrate this point: companies with real estate holdings abroad financed by local currency mortgages found that under FAS 8 their earnings were subject to considerable translation losses and gains. This came about because the value of their assets remained constant, as they were carried on the books at historical cost and translated at historical exchange rates, while the value of their local currency liabilities increased or decreased with every twitch of the exchange rate between reporting dates.

In contrast, U.S. companies whose foreign affiliates produced internationally traded goods (minerals or oil, for example) felt very comfortable valuing their assets on a dollar basis. Indeed, this later category of companies were the ones that did not like the transition to the *current/current* method at all. Here, all assets and liabilities are translated at the exchange rate prevailing on the reporting date. They found the underlying assumption that the value of all assets (denominated in the local currency of the given foreign affiliate) would change in direct proportion to the exchange rate change did not reflect the economic realities of their business.

In order to accommodate the conflicting requirements of companies in different situations and still maintain a semblance of conformity and comparability, at the end of 1981 the FASB issued Standard 52, replacing Standard 8. *FAS 52,* as it is commonly referred to, uses the current/current method as the basic translation rule. At the same time it mitigates the consequences by allowing companies to move translation losses directly to a special subaccount in the net worth section of the balance sheet, instead of adjusting current income. This latter provision may be viewed as a mere gimmick without much substance, providing at best a signalling function, indicating to users of accounting information that translation gains and losses are of a nature different from items normally found in income statements.

A more significant innovation of FAS 52 is the "functional" currency concept, which gives a company the opportunity to identify the primary economic environment and select the appropriate (functional) currency for each of the corporation's foreign entities. This approach reflects the official recognition by the accounting profession that the *location* of an entity does *not necessarily* indicate the currency relevant for a particular business. Thus FAS 52 represents an attempt to take into account the fact that exchange rate changes affect different companies in different ways, and that rigid and general rules treating different circumstances in the same manner will provide misleading information.

In order to adjust to the diversity of real life, FAS 52 had to become quite complex. The following discussion provides a brief road map to the logic of that standard.

In applying FAS 52 a company and its accountants must make two decisions in sequence. First, they must determine the functional currency of the entity whose accounts are to be consolidated. For all practical purposes, the choice here is between local currency and the U.S. dollar. In essence, there are a number of specific criteria which provide guidelines for this determination. As usual, extreme cases are relatively easily classified: a foreign affiliate engaged in retailing local goods and services will have the local currency as its functional currency, while a "border plant" that receives the majority of its inputs from abroad and ships the bulk of the output outside of the host country will have the dollar as its functional currency. If the functional currency is the dollar, foreign currency items on its balance sheet will have to be restated into dollars and any gains and losses are moved through the income statement, just as under FAS 8. If, on the other hand, the functional currency is determined to be the local currency, a second issue arises: whether or not the entity operates in a high inflation environment. High inflation countries are defined as those whose cumulative three-year inflation rate exceeds 100 percent. In that case, essentially the same principles as in FAS 8 are followed. In the case where the cumulative inflation rate falls short of 100 percent, the foreign affiliate's books are to be translated using the current exchange rate for all items, and any gains or losses are to go directly as a charge or credit to the equity accounts.

FAS 52 has a number of other fairly complex provisions regarding the treatment of hedge contracts, the definition of transactional gains and losses, and the accounting for intercompany transactions.

In essence, FAS 52 allows management much more flexibility to present the impact of exchange rate variations in accordance with perceived economic reality; by the same token, it provides greater scope for manipulation of reported earnings and it reduces comparability of financial data for different firms.

(c) Critique of the Accounting Model of Exposure.   Even with the increased flexibility of FAS 52, users of accounting information must be aware that there are three system sources of error that can mislead those responsible for exchange risk management (Adler, 1982):

1. Accounting data do not capture all commitments of the firm that give rise to exchange risk.
2. Because of the historical cost principle, accounting values of assets and liabilities do not reflect the respective contribution to total expected net cashflow of the firm.
3. Translation rules do not distinguish between expected and unexpected exchange rate changes.

Regarding the first point, it must be recognized that normally, commitments entered into by the firm in terms of foreign exchange, a purchase or a sales contract, for example, will not be booked until the merchandise has been shipped. At best, such obligations are shown as contingent liabilities. More importantly, accounting data reveals very little about the ability of the firm to change costs, prices and markets quickly. Alternatively, the firm may be committed by strategic decisions such as investment in plant and facilities. Such "commitments" are important criteria in determining the existence and magnitude of exchange risk.

The second point surfaced in our discussion of the temporal method: whenever asset values differ from market values, translation—however sophisticated—will not redress this original shortcoming. Thus, many of the perceived problems of FAS 8 had their roots not so much in translation, but in the fact that in an environment of inflation and exchange rate changes, the lack of current value accounting frustrates the best translation efforts.

Finally, translation rules do not take account of the fact that exchange rate changes have two components: (1) *expected* changes that are already reflected in the prices of assets and the costs of liabilities (relative interest rates); and (2) the *unexpected* deviations from the expected change which constitute the true sources of risk. The significance of this distinction is clear: economic decision makers have already taken account of expected changes; risk management efforts must focus on the effect of unexpected changes, as expected changes are reflected in prevailing prices and costs.

Many of the concepts touched upon in this section will become clearer as the discussion turns to an alternative way to measure corporate foreign exchange exposure.

(d) Economic Exposure.   The concept of economic exposure derives directly from the nature of the (nonfinancial) firm. Management in its entrepreneurial function perceives opportunities to generate profits, that is, expected positive net cashflows. These net cashflows, however, are often subject to (unexpected) exchange rate changes. Since the firm claims its special expertise in the exploitation of opportunities in the markets for *real goods and services,* the basic rationale for corporate foreign exchange exposure management is to shield net cashflows, and thus the value of the enterprise, from unanticipated exchange rate changes.

This thumbnail sketch of the economic foreign exchange exposure concept has a number of significant implications, some of which seem to be at variance with frequently used ideas in the popular literature and apparent practices in business firms. Specifically, there are implications regarding (1) the question of whether exchange risk originates from monetary or non-monetary transactions, (2) a reevaluation of traditional perspectives such as "transactions risk," and (3) the role of forecasting exchange rates in the context of corporate foreign exchange risk management.

(e) Contractual versus Noncontractual Returns.   An assessment of the nature of the firm's assets and liabilities and their respective cashflows shows that some are contractual, that is, fixed in nominal, monetary terms. Such returns, earnings from fixed interest securities and receivables, for example, and the negative returns on various liabilities are relatively easy to analyze with respect to exchange rate changes: when they are denominated in terms of foreign currency, their terminal value changes directly in proportion to the exchange rate change. Thus, with respect to financial items, the firm is concerned only about *net* assets or liabilities denominated in foreign currency, to the extent that maturities (actually, "durations" of asset classes) are matched.

What is much more difficult, however, is to gauge the impact on an exchange rate change on assets with noncontractual returns. While conventional discussions of exchange risk focus almost exclusively on financial assets, for trading and manufacturing firms at least, such assets are relatively less important than others. Indeed, equipment, real estate, buildings and inventories make the decisive contribution to the total cashfow of those firms. (Indeed companies frequently sell financial assets to banks, factors, or "captive" finance companies in order to leave banking to bankers and instead focus on the management of core assets!) And returns on such assets are affected in quite complex ways by changes in exchange rates. The most essential consideration is how the prices and costs of the firm will react in response to an unexpected exchange rate change. For example, if prices and costs react immediately and fully to offset exchange rate changes, the firm's cashflows are not exposed to exchange risk since they will not be affected in terms of the base currency. Thus, the value of noncontractual assets is not affected.

Inventories may serve as a good illustration of this proposition. The value of an inventory in a foreign subsidiary is determined not only by changes in the exchange rate, but also by a subsequent price change of the product—to the extent that the underlying *cause* of this price change is the exchange rate change. Thus, the dollar value of an inventory destined for export may increase when the currency of the destination country appreciates, provided its local currency prices do not decrease by the full percentage of the appreciation. Exhibit 27A.4 provides a numerical illustration.

The effect on the local currency price depends, in part, on competition in the market. The behavior of foreign and local competitors, in turn, depends on capacity utilization, market share objectives, likelihood of cost adjustments and a host of other factors. Of course, firms are not only interested in the value change or the behavior of cashflows of a single asset, but rather in the behavior of all cashflows. Again, price and cost adjustments need to be analyzed. For example, a firm that requires raw materials from abroad for production will usually find its stream of cash outlays going up when its local currency depreciates against foreign currencies. Yet the depreciation may cause foreign suppliers to lower prices in terms of foreign currencies for the purpose of maintaining market share.

(f) Currency of Denomination versus Currency of Determination.   One of the central concepts of modern international corporate finance is the distinction between the currency in which cashflows are *denominated* and the currency that *determines* the size of the cashflows. In the example in the previous section, it does not matter whether, as a matter of business practice, the firm may contract, be invoiced in, and pay for each individual shipment in its own local currency. If foreign exporters do not provide price concessions, the cash outflow of the importer behaves just like a foreign currency cashflow; even though payments are made in local currency, they occur in greater amounts. As a result, the cashflow, even while *denominated* in local currency, is *determined* by the relative value of the foreign currency. The functional currency concept introduced in FAS 52 is similar to the "currency of determination"—but not exactly. The currency of determination refers to revenue and operating expense flows, respectively; the functional currency concept pertains to an entity as a whole, and is, therefore, less precise.

To complicate things further, the *currency of recording,* that is, the currency in which the accounting records are kept, is yet another matter. For example, any debt contracted by the firm in foreign currency will always be recorded in the currency of the country where the corporate entity is *located.* However, the value of its legal obligation is established in the currency in which the contract is denominated.

ACCOUNTING VS. ECONOMIC EXPOSURE: INVENTORY

Assume the French sub of a U.S. corp. has an inventory destined for sale to Germany. Exchange rates are as follows:

before devaluation 1 FF = .15$ = .30 DM

after devaluation 1 FF = .12$ = .20 DM

Assumed "Passthrough" (in Percent)	Selling Price in Germany DM		Econ. Value of Inventory				Acct. Value (FIFO) in			
			FFR		$		France		the U.S.	
	Before	After	Before	After	Before	After	Before	After	Before	After
0	150	150	500[a]	750[b]	75	90	500[c]	500[c]	75	60
50	150	125	500	625	75	75	500	500	75	60
100	150	100	500	500	75	60	50	500	75	60

[a] 500 = 15 ÷ .30.
[b] 750 = 150 ÷ .20.
[c] Cost-of-goods-sold is assumed to be constant during the period.

Exhibit 27A.4.   Economic exposure, accounting exposure, and inventories: an illustration.

What does the effect of exchange rate changes on operational cash flows depend on?

1. *Volume Effects* (compensates for changes in profit margins).
2. *Pricing Flexibility* (change in margins to offset effect of exchange rate change).
3. *Diversification* of markets for inputs and outputs.
4. *Production and Sales Flexibility* (ability to shift markets and sources quickly).

It is possible, therefore, that a firm selling in export markets may record assets and liabilities in its local currency and invoice periodic shipments in a foreign currency and yet, if prices in the market are dominated by transactions in a third country, the cashflows received may behave as if they were in that third currency. To illustrate: A Brazilian firm selling coffee to West Germany may keep its records in cruzeiros, invoice in DMs, and have DM-denominated receivables, and physically collect DM cashflow, only to find that its revenue stream behaves as if it were in U.S. dollars! This occurs because DM-prices for each consecutive shipment are adjusted to reflect world market prices which, in turn, tend to be determined in U.S. dollars. The significance of this distinction is that the currency of denomination is (relatively) readily subject to management discretion, through the choice of invoicing currency. Prices and cash-flows, however, are determined by competitive conditions which are beyond the immediate control of the firm.

Yet an additional dimension of exchange risk involves the element of *time*. In the very short run, virtually all local currency prices for real goods and services (although not necessarily for financial assets) remain unchanged after an unexpected exchange rate change. However, over a longer period of time, prices and costs move inversely to spot rate changes; the tendency is for Purchasing Power Parity and the Law of One Price to hold.

In reality, this price adjustment process takes place over a great variety of time patterns. These patterns depend not only on the products involved, but also on market structure, the nature of competition, general business conditions, government policies such as price controls, and a number of other factors. Considerable work has been done on the phenomenon of "pass-through" of price changes caused by (unexpected) exchange rate changes.[1] And yet, because all the factors that determine the extent and speed of pass-through are very firm-specific and can be analyzed only on a case-by-case basis at the level of the operating entity of the firm (or strategic business unit), generalizations remain difficult to make. Exhibit 27A.5 summarizes the firm-specific effects of exchange rate changes on operating cash flows.

Conceptually, it is important to determine the time frame within which the firm cannot react to (unexpected) rate changes by (1) raising prices; (2) changing markets for inputs and outputs; and/or (3) adjusting production and sales volumes. Sometimes, at least one of these reactions is possible within a relatively short time; at other times, the firm is "locked in" through contractual or strategic commitments extending considerably into the future. Indeed, those firms which are free to react instantaneously and fully to adverse (unexpected) rate changes are not subject to exchange risk.

A further implication of the time-frame element is that exchange risk stems from the firm's position when its cashflows are, for a significant period, exposed to (unexpected) exchange rate changes, rather than the risk resulting from any specific international involvement. Thus, companies engaged purely in domestic transactions but who have dominant foreign competitors may feel the effect of exchange rate changes in their cashflows as much or even more than some firms that are actively engaged in exports, imports, or foreign direct investment.

---

[1] For a review of the literature see R. Naumann-Etienne, "A Framework for Financial Decisions in Multinational Corporations—A Summary of Recent Research," *Journal of Financial and Quantitative Analysis,* November 1974, pp. 859–874; and more recently Maurice Levi, *Financial Management and the International Economy* (New York: McGraw-Hill, 1983), Ch. 13.

WHAT IS ECONOMIC EXPOSURE?

PDVSA, the Venezuelan state-owned oil company, recently set up an oil refinery near Rotterdam, The Netherlands for shipment to Germany and other continental European countries. The firm planned to invoice its clients in ECU, the official currency unit of the European Community. The treasurer is considering sources of long term financing. In the past all long term finance was provided by the parent company, but working capital required to pay local salaries and expenses has been financed in Dutch guilders. The treasurer is not sure whether the short term debt should be hedged, or what currency to issue long term debt in.

This is an example of a situation where the definition of exposure has a direct impact on the firm's hedging decisions.

Translation exposure has to do with the *location of the assets,* which in this case would be a totally misleading measure of the effect of exchange rate changes on the value of the unit. After all, the oil comes from Venezuela and is shipped to Germany: its temporary resting place, be it a refinery in Rotterdam or a tanker en route to Germany, has no import. Both provide value added, but neither determine the currency of revenues. So financing should definitely not be done in Dutch guilders.

Transactions exposure has to do with the *currency of denomination* of assets like accounts receivable or payable. Once sales to Germany have been made and invoicing in ECU has taken place, PDVSA-Netherlands has contractual, ECU-denominated assets that should be financed or hedged with ECU. For future sales, however, PDVSA-Netherlands does not have exposure to the ECU. This is because the currency of determination is the U.S. dollar.

Economic exposure is tied to the *currency of determination* of revenues and costs. Since the world market price of oil is dollars, this is the effective currency in which PDVSA's future sales to Germany are made. If the ECU rises against the dollar, PDVSA must adjust its ECU price down to match those of competitors like Aramco. If the dollar rises against the ECU, PDVSA can and should raise prices to keep the dollar price the same, since competitors would do likewise. Clearly the currency of determination is influenced by the currency in which competitors denominate prices.

The conclusion is, therefore, that the Dutch subsidiary of a Venezuelan company whose sales to Germany are invoiced in ECU should do its long term financing in U.S. dollars, to hedge the effective currency of exposure.

Exhibit 27A.5. Exposure concepts: Currency of Location vs. Currency of Denomination vs. Currency of Determination.

27A.5 MANAGING ECONOMIC EXPOSURE

(a) Economic Effects of Unanticipated Exchange Rate Changes on Cash Flows.   From this analytical framework, some practical implications emerge for the assessment of economic exposure. First, the firm must project its cost and revenue streams over a planning horizon that represents the period of time during which the firm is "locked-in," or constrained from reacting to (unexpected) exchange rate changes. It must then assess the impact of a deviation of the actual exchange rate from the rate used in the projection of costs and revenues.

Subsequently, the effects on the various cashflows of the firm must be netted over product lines and markets to account for diversification effects where gains and losses could cancel out, wholly or in part. The remaining net loss or gain is the subject of economic exposure management. For a multiunit, multiproduct, multinational corporation the net exposure may not be very large at all because of the many offsetting effects. By contrast, enterprises that have invested in the development of one or two major foreign markets are typically subject to considerable fluctuations of their net cashflows, regardless of whether they invoice in their own or in the foreign currency.

For practical purposes, three questions capture the extent of a company's foreign exchange exposure.

1. How quickly can the firm adjust prices to offset the impact of an unexpected exchange rate change on profit margins?

2. How quickly can the firm change sources for inputs and markets for outputs? Or, alternatively, how diversified are a company's factor and product markets?

3. To what extent do volume changes, associated with unexpected exchange rate changes, have an impact on the value of assets?

Normally, the executives within business firms who can supply the best estimates on these issues tend to be those directly involved with purchasing, marketing, and production. Finance managers who focus exclusively on credit and foreign exchange markets may easily miss the essence of corporate foreign exchange risk.

(b) Financial versus Operating Strategies for Hedging.   When operating (cash) inflows and (contractual) outflows from liabilities are affected by exchange rate changes, the general principle of prudent exchange risk management is: any effect on cash inflows and outflows should cancel out as much as possible. This can be achieved by maneuvering assets, liabilities, or both. When should operations—the asset side—be used?

Exchange rate changes can have tremendous effects on operating cash flows; it makes sense, therefore, to adjust operations to hedge against these effects. Many companies, such as Japanese auto producers, are now seeking flexibility in production location, in part to be able to respond to large and persistent exchange rate changes that make production much cheaper in one location than another. Among the operating policies are the shifting of markets for output, sources of supply, product-lines, and production facilities as a defensive reaction to adverse exchange rate changes. Put differently, deviations from purchasing power parity provide profit opportunities for the operations-flexible firm. This philosophy is epitomized in the following quotation.

> It has often been joked at Philips that in order to take advantage of currency movements, it would be a good idea to put our factories aboard a supertanker, which could put down anchor wherever exchange rates enable the company to function most efficiently. . . In the present currency markets. . . [this] would certainly not be a suitable means of transport for taking advantage of exchange rate movements. An aeroplane would be more in line with the requirements of the present era.[2]

The problem is that Philips' production could not fit into either craft. It is obvious that such measures will be very costly, especially if undertaken over a short span of time. It follows that operating policies are *not* the tools of choice for exchange risk management. Hence operating policies which have been designed to reduce or eliminate exposure will only be undertaken as a last resort, when less expensive options have been exhausted.

It is not surprising, therefore, that exposure *management* focuses not on the asset side, but primarily on the liability side of the firm's balance sheet. The steps involved in managing economic exposure are summarized as:

1. Estimation of planning horizon as determined by reaction period.

2. Determination of expected future spot rate.

3. Estimation of expected revenue and cost streams, given the expected spot rate.

4. Estimation of effect on revenue and expense streams for unexpected exchange rate changes.

---

[2] D. Snijders, "Global Company and World Financial Markets," in *Financing the World Economy in the Nineties,* J.J. Sijben, ed. (Dordrecht, Netherlands: Kluwer Academic Publishers, 1989).

5. Choice of appropriate currency for debt denomination.

6. Estimation of necessary amount of foreign currency debt.

7. Determination of average interest period of debt.

8. Selection between direct or indirect debt denomination.

9. Decision on trade-off between arbitrage gains vs. exchange risk stemming from exposure in markets where rates are distorted by controls.

10. Decision about "residual" risk: consider adjusting business strategy.

Whether and how these steps should be implemented depends first, on the extent to which the firm wishes to rely on currency forecasting to make hedging decisions, and second, on the range of hedging tools available and their suitability to the task. These issues are addressed in the next two sections.

27A.6 GUIDELINES FOR CORPORATE FORECASTING OF EXCHANGE RATES. Academics and practitioners have sought the determinants of exchange rate changes ever since there were currencies. Many students have learned about the balance of trade and how the more a country exports, the more demand there is for its currency, and so the stronger is its exchange rate. In practice, the story is a lot more complex. Research in the foreign exchange markets have come a long way since the days when international trade was thought to be the dominant factor determining the level of the exchange rate. Monetary variables, capital flows, rational expectations and portfolio balance are all now understood to factor into the determination of currencies in a floating exchange rate system. Many models have been developed to explain and to forecast exchange rates. No model has yet proved to be the definitive one, perhaps because the structure of the worlds economies and financial markets are undergoing such rapid evolution.

Corporations nevertheless avidly seek ways to predict currencies, in order to decide when and when not to hedge. The models they use typically entail one or more of the following kinds: *political event analysis,* or *fundamental,* or *technical.*

Academic students of international finance, in contrast, find strong empirical support for the role of arbitrage in global financial markets, and for the view that exchange rates exhibit behavior that is characteristic of other speculative asset markets. Exchange rates react quickly to news. Rates are far more volatile than changes in underlying economic variables; they are moved by changing expectations, and hence are difficult to forecast. In a broad sense they are "efficient," but tests of efficiency face inherent obstacles in testing the precise nature of this efficiency directly.

The central "efficient market" model is the *unbiased forward rate theory* introduced earlier. It says that the forward rate equals the expected future level of the spot rate. Because the forward rate is a contractual price, it offers opportunities for speculative profits for those who correctly assess the future spot price relative to the current forward rate. Specifically, *risk neutral* players will seek to make a profit if their forecast differs from the forward rate, so if there are enough such participants the forward rate will always be bid up or down until it equals the expected future spot. Because expectations of future spot rates are formed on the basis of presently available information (historical data) and an interpretation of its implication for the future, they tend to be subject to frequent and rapid revision. The actual future spot rate may therefore deviate markedly from the expectation embodied in the present forward rate for that maturity. *The actual exchange rate may deviate from the expected by some random error.*

As is indicated in Exhibit 27A.6, in an efficient market, the forecasting error will be distributed randomly, according to some probability distribution, with a mean equal to zero. An implication of this is that today's forecast, as represented by the forward rate, is equal to yesterday's forward plus some random amount. In other words, the forward rate itself follows

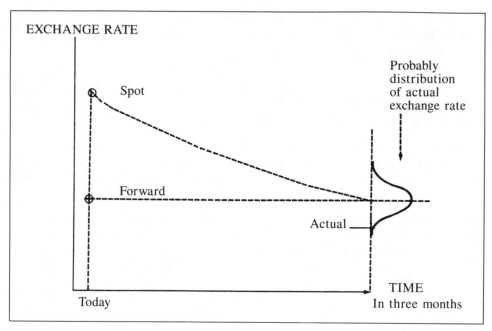

Exhibit 27A.6.   The unbiased forward rate theory.

a random walk.[3] Another way of looking at these errors to consider them as speculative profits or losses: what you would gain or lose if you consistently bet against the forward rate. Can they be consistently positive or negative? A priori reasoning suggests that this should not be the case. Otherwise one would have to explain why consistent losers do not quit the market, or why consistent winners are not imitated by others or do not increase their volume of activity, thus causing adjustment of the forward rate in the direction of their expectation. Barring such explanation, one would expect that the forecast error is sometimes positive, sometimes negative, alternating in a random fashion, driven by unexpected events in the economic and political environment.

Rigorously tested academic models have cast doubt on the pure unbiased forward rate theory of efficiency, and demonstrated the presence of speculative profit opportunities (for example, by the use of "filter rules"). However it is also logical to suppose that speculators will bear foreign exchange risk only if they are compensated with a risk premium. Are the above-zero expected returns excessive in a risk-adjusted sense? Given the small size of the bias in the forward exchange market, and the magnitude of daily currency fluctuations, the answer is "probably not."

As a result of their finding that the foreign exchange markets are among the world's most efficient, academics argue the exchange rate forecasting by corporations, in the sense of trying to beat the market, plays a role only under very special circumstances. Few firms actively decide to commit real assets in order to take currency positions. Rather, they get involved with foreign currencies in the course of pursuing profits from the exploitation of a competitive advantage; rather than being based on currency expectations, this advantage is based on expertise

---

[3] Note that when we say the forward rate follows a random walk, we mean the forward rate for a given delivery date, not the rolling 3-month forward. Since the only published measure of a forward rate for a given delivery date is the price of a futures contract, the latter serves as a proxy to test the proposition that the forward rate should fluctuate randomly.

in such areas as production, marketing, the organization of people, or other technical resources. If someone does have special expertise in forecasting foreign exchange rates, such skills can usually be put to use without incurring the risks and costs of committing funds to other than purely financial assets. Most finance managers of nonfinancial enterprises concentrate on producing and selling goods; they should find themselves acting as speculative foreign exchange traders only because of an occasional opportunity encountered in the course of their normal operations. Only when foreign exchange markets are systematically distorted by government controls on financial institutions do the operations of trading and manufacturing firms provide an opportunity to move funds and gain from purely financial transactions.

Forecasting exchange rate changes, however, *is* important for planning purposes. To the extent that all significant managerial tasks are concerned with the future, anticipated exchange rate changes are a major input into virtually *all* decisions of enterprises involved in and affected by international transactions. However, the task of forecasting foreign exchange rates for planning and decision-making purposes, with the purpose of determining the most likely exchange rate, is quite different from attempting to beat the market in order to derive speculative profits.

Expected exchange rate changes are revealed by market prices when rates are free to reach their competitive levels. Organized futures or forward markets provide inexpensive information regarding future exchange rates, using the best available data and judgment. Thus, whenever profit-seeking, well-informed traders can take positions, forward rates, prices of future contracts, and interest differentials for instruments of similar riskiness (but denominated in different currencies), provide good indicators of expected exchange rates. In this fashion, an input for corporate planning and decision-making is readily available in all currencies where there are no effective exchange controls. The advantage of such market-based rates over "in-house" forecast is that they are both less expensive and more likely to be accurate. Market rates are determined by those who tend to have the best information and track-record; incompetent market participants lose money and are eliminated.

The nature of this market-based expected exchange rate should not lead to confusing notions about the accuracy of prediction. In speculative markets, all decisions are made on the basis of interpretation of past data; however, new information surfaces constantly. Therefore, market-based forecasts rarely will come true. The actual price of a currency will either be below or above the rate expected by the market. If the market knew which would be more likely, any predictive bias quickly would be corrected. Any predictable, economically meaningful bias would be corrected by the transactions of profit-seeking transactors.

The importance of market-based forecasts for a determination of the foreign exchange exposure of the firm is that of a benchmark against which the economic consequences of deviations must be measured. This can be put in the form of a concrete question: How will the expected net cashflow of the firm behave if the future spot exchange rate is *not* equal to the rate predicted by the market when commitments are made? The nature of this kind of forecast is completely different from trying to outguess the foreign exchange markets.[4]

27A.7 TOOLS AND TECHNIQUES FOR THE MANAGEMENT OF FOREIGN EXCHANGE RISK.   In this section we consider the relative merits of several different tools for hedging exchange risk, including forward, futures, debt, swaps, and options. We will use the following criteria for contrasting the tools.

First, there are different tools that serve effectively the same purpose. Most currency management instruments enable the firm to take a long or a short position to hedge an opposite short or long position. Thus one can hedge a DM payment using forward exchange contract, or debt in DM, or futures or perhaps a currency swap. In equilibrium the cost of all will be the

---

[4] See Gunter Dufey and Ian H. Giddy, "International Financial Planning: The Use of Market-Based Forecasts," *California Management Review*, XXI, 1 (Fall 1978), pp. 69–81.

same, according to the fundamental relationships of the international money market as illustrated in Exhibit 27A.1. They differ in details like default risk or transactions costs, of if there is some fundamental market imperfection. Indeed in an efficient market one would expect *anticipated* cost of hedging to be zero. This follows from the unbiased forward rate theory.

Second, tools differ in that they hedge different risks. In particular, symmetric hedging tools like futures cannot easily hedge contingent cash flows: options may be better suited to the latter.

(a) Tools and Techniques: Foreign Exchange Forwards.

Foreign exchange is the exchange of one currency for another. Trading or "dealing" in each pair of currencies consists of two parts, *the spot market,* where payment (delivery) is made right away (in practice this means usually the second business day), and *the forward market.* The rate in the forward market is a price for foreign currency set at the time the transaction is agreed to but with the actual exchange, or delivery, taking place at a specified time in the future. While the amount of the transaction, the value date, the payments procedure, and the exchange rate are all determined in advance, *no exchange of money takes place until the actual settlement date.* This commitment to exchange currencies at a previously agreed exchange rate is usually referred to as a *forward contract.*

Forward contracts are the most common means of hedging transactions in foreign currencies, for example:

> J. Fredericks, Foreign Exchange Manager at Murray Chemical, was informed that Murray was selling 25,000 tonnes of naphtha to Canada for a total price of C$11,500,000, to be paid upon delivery in two months' time. To protect his company, he arranged to sell 11.5 million Canadian dollars *forward* to the Royal Bank of Montreal. The two-month forward contract price was US$0.8785 per Canadian dollar. Two months and two days later, Fredericks received US$10,102,750 from RBM and paid RBM C$11,500,000, the amount received from Murray's customer.

The trouble with forward contracts, however, is that they require future performance, and sometimes one party is unable to perform on the contract. When that happens, the hedge disappears, sometimes at great cost to the hedger. This default risk also means that many companies do not have access to the forward market in sufficient quantity to fully hedge their exchange exposure. For such situations, futures may be more suitable.

(b) Currency Futures.

Outside of the interbank forward market, the best-developed market for hedging exchange rate risk is the *currency futures* market. In principle, currency futures are similar to foreign exchange forwards in that they are contracts for delivery of a certain amount of a foreign currency at some future date and at a known price. In practice, they differ from forward contracts in important ways.

One difference between forwards and futures is standardization. Forwards are for any amount, as long as it's big enough to be worth the dealer's time, while futures are for standard amounts, each contract being far smaller than the average forward transaction. Futures are also standardized in terms of delivery date. The normal currency futures delivery dates are March, June, September and December, while forwards are private agreements that can specify any delivery date that the parties choose. Both of these features allow the futures contract to be tradable.

Another difference is that forwards are traded by phone and telex and are completely independent of location or time. Futures, on the other hand, are traded in organized exchanges such as the LIFFE in London, SIMEX in Singapore and the IMM in Chicago. But the most important feature of the futures contract is not its standardization or trading organization but in the *time pattern of the cash flows* between parties to the transaction. In a forward contract, whether it involves full delivery of the two currencies or just compensation of the net value, the transfer of funds takes place once: at maturity. With futures, cash changes hands every day during the life of the contract, or at least every day that has seen a change in the price of the contract. *This daily cash compensation feature largely eliminates default risk.*

Thus forwards and futures serve similar purposes, and tend to have identical rates, but differ in their applicability. Most big companies use forwards; futures tend to be used whenever credit risk may be a problem.

(c) Debt Instead of Forwards or Futures.   Debt—borrowing in the currency to which the firm is exposed or investing in interest-bearing assets to offset a foreign currency payment—is a widely used hedging tool that serves much the same purpose as forward contracts.

In our example, Fredericks sold Canadian dollars forward. Alternatively she could have used the Eurocurrency market to achieve the same objective. She would borrow Canadian dollars, which she would then change into francs in the spot market, and hold them in a U.S. dollar deposit for two months. When payment in Canadian dollars was received from the customer, she would use the proceeds to pay down the Canadian dollar debt. Such a transaction is termed a *money market hedge.*

The cost of this money market hedge is the difference between the Canadian dollar interest rate paid and the U.S. dollar interest rate earned. According to the *interest rate parity theorem,* the interest differential equals the forward exchange premium, the percentage by which the forward rate differs from the spot exchange rate. So the cost of the money market hedge should be the same as the forward or futures market hedge, unless the firm has some advantage in one market or the other.

The money market hedge suits many companies because they have to borrow anyway, so it simply is a matter of denominating the company's debt in the currency to which it is exposed. That is logical. But if a money market hedge is to be done for its own sake, as in the example just given, the firm ends up borrowing from one bank and lending to another, thus losing on the spread. This is costly, so the forward hedge would probably be more advantageous except where the firm had to borrow for ongoing purposes anyway.

(d) Currency Options.   Many companies, banks and governments have extensive experience in the use of forward exchange contracts. With a forward contract one can lock in an exchange rate for the future. There are a number of circumstances, however, where it may be desirable to have more flexibility than a forward provides. For example, a computer manufacturer in California may have sales priced in U.S. dollars as well as in German marks in Europe. Depending on the relative strength of the two currencies, revenues may be realized in either German marks or dollars. In such a situation the use of forward or futures would be inappropriate: there's no point in hedging something you might not have. What is called for is a foreign exchange option: the right, but not the obligation, to exchange currency at a predetermined rate.

A foreign exchange option in a contract for future delivery of a currency in exchange for another, where the holder of the option has the right to buy (or sell) the currency at an agreed price, the *strike* or exercise price, but is not required to do so. The right to buy is a *call;* the right to sell, a *put.* For such a right he pays a price called the *option premium.* The option seller receives the premium and is obliged to make (or take) delivery at the agreed-upon price if the buyer exercises his option. In some options, the instrument being delivered is the currency itself; in others, a futures contract on the currency. *American options* permit the holder to exercise at any time before the expiration date; *European options,* only on the expiration date.

The following example illustrates the lopsided character of options. Futures and forwards are contracts in which two parties oblige themselves to exchange something in the future. They are thus useful to hedge or convert known currency or interest rate exposures. An option, in contrast, gives one party the *right but not the obligation* to buy or sell an asset under specified conditions while the other party *assumes an obligation* to sell or buy that asset if that option is exercised.

Steve Parker of Campbell Soup had just agreed to purchase I£5 million worth of potatoes from his supplier in County Cork, Ireland. Payment of the five million punt was to be made in 245 days' time. The dollar had recently plummeted against all the EMS currencies and Parker wanted to avoid any further rise in the cost of imports. He viewed the dollar as being extremely unstable in the current environment of economic tensions. Having decided to hedge the payment, he had obtained dollar/punt quotes of $2.25 spot, $2.19 for 245 days forward delivery. His view, however, was that the dollar was bound to rise in the next few months, so he was strongly considering purchasing a call option instead of buying the punt forward. At a strike price of $2.21, the best quote he had been able to obtain was from the Ballad Bank of Dublin, who would charge a premium of 0.85% of the principal.

Parker decided to buy the call option. In effect, he reasoned, I'm paying for downside protection while not limiting the possible savings I could reap if the dollar does recover to a more realistic level. In a highly volatile market where crazy currency values can be reached, options make more sense than taking your chances in the market, and you're not locked into a rock-bottom forward rate.

When should a company like Campbell use options in preference to forwards or futures? In the example, Parker had a view on the currency's *direction* that differed from the forward rate. Taken alone, this would suggest taking a position. But he also had a view on the dollar's *volatility*. As we will explain later on, options provide the only convenient means of hedging or positioning "volatility risk." Indeed the price of an option is directly influenced by the outlook for a currency's volatility: the more volatile, the higher the price. To Parker, the price is worth paying. In other words he thinks the true volatility is greater than that reflected in the option's price.

* This example highlights one set of circumstances under which a company should consider the use of options. A currency call or put option's value is affected by *both* direction and volatility changes, and the price of such an option will be higher, the more the market's expectations (as reflected in the forward rate) favor exercise and the greater the anticipated volatility. For example, during the crisis in the European Monetary System of mid-1993, put options on the French franc became very expensive for two reasons. First, high French interest rates designed to support the franc drove the forward rate to a discount against the German mark. Second, anticipated volatility of the DM/FF exchange rate jumped as dealers speculated on a possible break-up of the EMS. With movements much greater than the EMS official bands possible, the expected gain from exercising puts became much greater. It was an appropriate time for companies with French exposure to buy puts, but the cost would exceed the expected gain unless the corporate Treasury anticipated a greater change, or an even higher volatility, than those reflected in the market price of options.

* Finally, one can justify the limited use of options by reference to the deleterious effect of *financial distress* alluded to in section 27A.2. Unmanaged exchange rate risk can cause significant fluctuations in the earnings and the market value of an international firm. A very large exchange rate movement may cause special problems for a particular company, perhaps because it brings a competitive threat from a different country. At some level, the currency change may threaten the firm's viability, bringing the costs of bankruptcy to bear. To avert this, it may be worth buying some low-cost options that would pay off only under unusual circumstances, ones that would particularly hurt the firm. Out-of-the-money options may be a useful and cost-effective way to hedge against currency risks that have very low probabilities but which, if they occur, have disproportionately high costs to the company.

* **27A.8 CONTROLLING CORPORATE TREASURY TRADING RISKS.** In a corporation, there is no such thing as being perfectly hedged. Not every transaction can be matched, for international trade and production is a complex and uncertain business. As we have seen, even identifying the correct currency of exposure, the currency of determination, is tricky. Flexibility is called for, and management must necessarily give some discretion, perhaps even a lot of discretion, to the corporate treasury department or whichever unit is charged with managing foreign exchange risks. Some companies, feeling that foreign exchange is best handled by

professionals, hire ex-bank dealers; others groom engineers or accountants. Yet however talented and honorable are these individuals, it has become evident that some limits must be imposed on the trading activities of the corporate treasury, for losses can get out of hand even in the best of companies.

In 1992 a *Wall Street Journal* reporter found that Dell Computer Corporation, a star of the retail PC industry, had been trading currency options with a face value that exceeded Dell's annual international sales, and that currency losses may have been covered up. Complex options trading was in part responsible for losses at the treasury of Allied-Lyons, the British foods group. The $150 million lost almost brought the company to its knees, and the publicity precipitated a management shake-out. In 1993 the oil giant Royal Dutch-Shell revealed that currency trading losses of as much as a billion dollars had been uncovered in its Japanese subsidiary.

Performance measurement standards, accountability and limits of some form must be part of a treasury foreign currency hedging program. Space does not permit a detailed examination of trading control methods, but some broad principles can be stated.

First, management must elucidate the goals of exchange risk management, preferably in operational terms rather than in platitudes such as "we hedge all foreign exchange risks."

Second, the risks of in-house trading (for that's often what it is) must be recognized. These include losses on open positions from exchange rate changes, counterparty credit risks, and operations risks.

Third, for all net positions taken, the firm must have an *independent* method of valuing, marking-to-market, the instruments traded. This marking to market need not be included in external reports, if the positions offset other exposures that are not marked to market, but is necessary to avert hiding of losses. Wherever possible, marking to market should be based on external, objective prices traded in the market.

Fourth, position limits should be made explicit rather than treated as "a problem we would rather not discuss." Instead of hamstringing treasury with a complex set of rules, limits can take the form of prohibiting positions that could incur a loss (or gain) beyond a certain amount, based on sensitivity analysis. As in all these things, any attempt to cover up losses should reap severe penalties.

Finally, counterparty risks resulting from over-the-counter forward or swap contracts should be evaluated in precisely the same manner as is done when the firm extends credit to, say, suppliers or customers.

In all this, the chief financial officer might well seek the assistance of an accounting or consulting firm, and may wish to purchase software tailored to the purposes.

27A.9 CONCLUSIONS.   This chapter offers an introduction to the complex subject of the measurement and management of foreign exchange risk. We began by noting some problems with interpretation of the concept, and entered the debate as to whether and why companies should devote active managerial resources to something that is so difficult to define and measure.

Accountants' efforts to put a static value on a firm involved in international business has led many to focus on the translated balance sheet as a target for hedging exposure. As was demonstrated, however, there are numerous realistic situations where the economic effect of exchange rate changes differ from those predicted by the various measures of translation exposure. In particular, we emphasized the distinctions between the currency of location, the currency of denomination, and the currency of determination of a business.

After giving some guidelines for the management of economic exposure, the chapter addressed the thorny question of how to approach currency forecasting. We suggested a market-based approach to international financial planning, and cast doubt on the corporation's treasury department to outguess the forward exchange rate.

The chapter then turned to the tools and techniques of hedging, contrasting the application that require forwards, futures, money market hedging, and currency options.

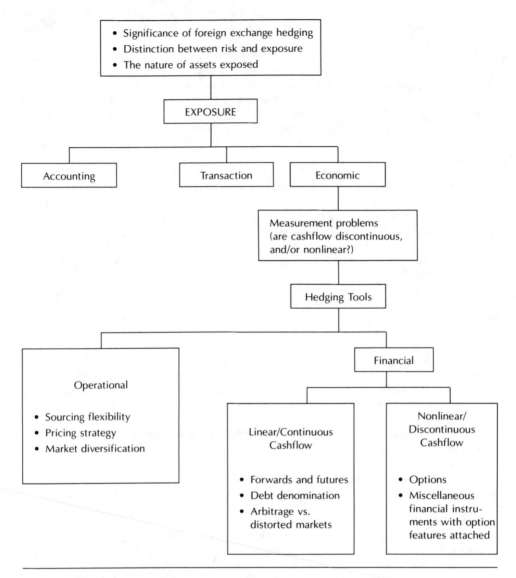

Exhibit 27A.7.   Management of Corporate Foreign Exchange Exposure.

In Exhibit 27A.7, we present a sketch of how a company may approach the exchange risk management task, based on the principles laid out in this chapter.

SOURCES AND SUGGESTED REFERENCES

Michael Alder. "Translation Methods and Operational Foreign Exchange Risk Management," Chap. 6 of Göran Bergendahl, ed., *International Financial Management,* Stockholm: Norstedts, 1982.

Robert Z. Aliber. *Exchange Risk and Corporate International Finance.* New York: John Wiley & Sons, 1979.

Bradford Cornell. "Inflation, Relative Price Changes, and Exchange Risk," *Financial Management,* Autumn 1980, pp. 30–44.

Gunter Dufey. "Corporate Finance and Exchange Rate Variations," *Financial Management,* Summer 1972, pp. 51–57.

Gunter Dufey and Ian Giddy. "International Financial Planning: The Use of Market-Based Forecasts," *California Management Review,* Fall 1978, pp. 69–81.

R. Dukes. *An Empirical Investigation of the Effects of Statement of Financial Accounting Standards No. 8 on Security Return Behavior.* Stamford, Conn: Financial Accounting Standards Board, 1978.

Mark R. Eaker. "The Numeraire Problem and Foreign Exchange Risk," *Journal of Finance,* May 1981, pp. 419–427.

George Feiger and Bertran Jacquillat. *International Finance: Text and Cases.* Boston: Allyn & Bacon, 1981.

Ian H. Giddy. "Why It Doesn't Pay to Make a Habit of Forward Hedging," *Euromoney,* December 1976, pp. 96–100.

Christine R. Hekman. "Foreign Exchange Exposure: Accounting Measures and Economic Reality," *Journal of Cash Management,* February/March 1983, pp. 34–45.

James E. Hodder. "Hedging International Exposure: Capital Structure Under Flexible Exchange Rates and Expropriation Risk," unpublished working paper, Stanford University, November 1982.

Laurent L. Jacque. "Management of Foreign Exchange Risk: A Review Article," *Journal of International Business Studies,* Spring/Summer 1981, pp. 81–101.

Donald R. Lessard. *International Financial Management.* Boston: Warren, Gorham and Lamont, 1979.

Maurice Levi. *Financial Management and the International Economy.* New York: McGraw-Hill, 1983.

Dennis E. Logue and George S. Oldfield. "Managing Foreign Assets When Foreign Exchange Markets are Efficient," *Financial Management,* Summer 1977, pp. 16–22.

John H. Makin. "Portfolio Theory and the Problem of Foreign Exchange Risks," *Journal of Finance,* May 1978, pp. 517–534.

MULTINATIONAL INFORMATION SYSTEMS (NEW)

Jon A. Turner

New York University

SUPPLEMENT CONTENTS

28A.1   INTRODUCTION

(a) Intended Audience.   This chapter is intended for professionals and managers interested in the use of information technology (IT) in multinational firms. Little knowledge of IT is assumed. Readers with a detailed knowledge of IT may wish to skip Appendixes A and B that describe primarily the technology.

(b) Role of Information Technology in the Management of Multinational Corporations.
Executives manage largely on the basis of information. Multinational managers typically require a greater quantity of more diverse information than do their domestic counterparts. This is because information from subsidiaries must (1) conform to both local and global needs, and (2) be qualified by particular knowledge of the context in which it has been gathered for it to be understood and aggregated.

Two factors govern the amount of information required to be transmitted between subsidiary and headquarters: the scope of business activity at the subsidiary and the decision authority of local managers. The greater the scope of activity at the subsidiary, the greater the amount of information transmitted to headquarters. Conversely, the greater the decision authority of local managers, the less information transmitted.

Information may be used for a variety of purposes that range from reporting to communication. It is useful to distinguish among three categories of information transmission: transactions, reports, and messages. Transactions are transmissions that describe basic business activity, such as a purchase order or an invoice. These are generated when the activity takes place (often at the subsidiary) and transmitted to where the information is processed (sometimes headquarters or a regional processing center). Reports are predetermined information groupings, such as a monthly statement, that are provided upon request. Reports may be either periodic in that they are produced at set intervals, or ad hoc where they are generated when needed. Messages are point to point information transmissions consisting of text, graphics, or video media sent over a network. Which media may be transmitted is determined by the characteristics of the network. Messages require the sender to know the network address of the recipient.

It is useful also to distinguish among the type of data that is transmitted. Three categories are important: corporate, local, and personal. Corporate data is official shared data that describes corporate activity. An example would be a monthly departmental accounting statement. Corporate data often comes from a corporate information (application) system, for example, the General Ledger or Human Resource System and implies that agreement has been reached across the corporation as to the exact meaning of the data in the system. In contrast, local data applies only to the organizational unit that generates it, for example, a report of the inventory level in a subsidiary's warehouse. Personal data refers to data generated by an individual, such as a client report or a spread sheet analysis. It is important for the recipient of a message to know the type of data contained in a message.

Regarding the importance of IT, Bartlett and Ghoshal (1989) observe that firms operating globally will be at a serious strategic disadvantage if they are unable to firmly control their worldwide operations and manage them in a globally coordinated manner.

28A.2 PERSPECTIVES ON INFORMATION SYSTEMS. Many types of systems are used in organizations. Three perspectives or views can be used to describe these systems: functional, informational, and systems.

(a) Functional View. Information systems often support a primary business function. Many of the requirements for a system can be established by identifying the particular function a system supports.

(i) Production. Information systems are used to maintain a product's Bill of Materials, to schedule production equipment, to control production equipment, and to track a product through the various phases of production. Systems are used also more directly in actual product design, a process called computer aided design (CAD).

(ii) Marketing and Sales. Analysis of sales data can be used to estimate future product production. For example, at the end of each business day Benetton retail stores report sales to headquarters. This information is used to monitor performance, as the basis for production planning, and to spot industry trends. Analysis of customer needs and preferences can be used for new product design. American Hospital Supply's order entry system was used effectively to tie purchasing departments of hospitals more closely to them and to boost the average number of items ordered and value of each order.

(iii) Logistics. Information systems are used to maintain track of inventory, parts for repair, and the location of goods being shipped. By being able to track the location of each object they handle, Federal Express has established a competitive advantage over their rivals.

(iv) Service and Support. Systems can be used to provide assistance to service operators. For example, ATT has developed automated systems to assist telephone operators in rapidly locating telephone numbers. And most software manufacturers provide on-line documentation, a problem log, and other information resources to assist their service personnel. Systems are used to track service requests. Otis Elevator established a service tracking system that was instrumental in identifying improperly designed parts and recognizing better performing service personnel.

(v) Human Resources. Systems are used to maintain personnel data, to determine employee benefit eligibility, for maintaining a skills inventory of a firm's staff, and for determining compensation.

(vi) Procurement. A firm may maintain a list of preferred vendors and be connected to them electronically for the purpose of order entry, or to an electronic network for competitive bidding.

(vii) Financial Management. Accounting data is used to determine the financial position of a firm, to monitor the performance of a subsidiary, and the cost of producing a product or service.

(viii) Infrastructure. Certain resources are required to build other systems. These include computers, applications development software, a data communications network, and a skilled development staff.

(b) Activity View.   Another perspective on a firm's systems follows the activities they per- form. This provides a view of the detailed information needs by activity.

(i) Collections.   These consist of credit control including the identification of major accounts outstanding, credit histories and the establishment of credit limits; accounts receivable includ- ing an intercompany aging report and major delinquency accounts; receipts including amounts collected by currency, projected collections by currency; and variance analysis of previous projections.

(ii) Disbursements.   These include order placement; raw materials inventory; payments; amounts paid by currency; projected disbursements by currency; and variance analysis.

(iii) Operating Expense.   Including forecasts of receipts and disbursements by currency; fore- casts of exports and imports by country; summary of all exposed positions and hedging actions taken; and variance analysis.

(iv) Liquidity.   These include borrowings outstanding; investments made; investment/borrow- ing opportunities with rates applied; forecasts of cash position; forecasts of interest rates; and variance analysis.

(v) Product Line Performance.   These consist of products produced in the period; hours worked by category by product; materials used by category by product; resources used by cate- gory by product; breakdown report indicating hours lost; quality report; projections for next period; and variance analysis.

(vi) Customer Profiling.   Analysis of customer profiles by product and region.

(vii) Competitor Analysis.   Competitor sales by product by region; comparative financial ratio analysis; forecasts for next period; trends; and variance analysis.

(c) Systems View.   A third way to classify systems is by their internal form.

(i) Organizational Level.   Systems may support workers at the operational level, the manage- ment control level, or the executive level of a firm. At the operational level, application systems perform tasks that clerical workers used to perform. For example, the posting of transactions to a ledger. Management control systems track the allocation and expenditure of resources and are used mostly by middle management. Systems that support executives are of two types. One is used for forecasting and environmental scanning. The other, called executive information sys- tems, aggregate key data on firm performance to keep executives informed.

(ii) Decision Type.   Since much of what workers do in business involves decision making, application systems may be seen as composed of many decisions (among other processing activ- ities). Decisions may be structured in that the procedure to be used in making them is well understood, for example, minimum order quantity in inventory replenishment. Or, decisions may be unstructured where the situation has not been encountered previously and the procedure for solution is unclear. An example of the latter would be a decision on whether to acquire a firm. In this case, considerable judgment and analysis is involved.

(iii) Data Content.   Data vary in a number of ways, including their accuracy, their level of detail, and their time orientation (that is, whether they pertain to the present, past, or future). When the data in a system is highly varied it increases the complexity of the system.

(iv) System Type.   Information systems can be divided into four types: operational systems, control systems, decision support systems, and infrastructure systems. Operational systems differ from other systems in that they tend to serve the operational level of a firm, consist mostly of structured decisions, and make use of data that is detailed, accurate, focused on internal operations, and pertains to past or current events. Operational systems process transactions and tend to be large, high activity systems, run continuously. They must be extremely accurate and reliable. Because of their size, performance is a key factor, and because they support major operations of the firm they need to be available continuously. Examples would be an airline reservation system, such as American Airline's SABRE. Should the system be down, agents around the world could not book flights. Most application systems in firms fall into this category and the rationale for them is often cost displacement.

Control systems support middle management in tracking and monitoring activities. They consist of more unstructured decisions than operational systems, use data about internal operations with a past or current orientation that is detailed and accurate. These systems tend to be smaller than operational systems and to be run periodically rather than continuously.

Decision support systems (DSS) provide direct support to decision makers, often executives or professionals, in some task. Executive support systems fall into this category. DSSs, which may be quite small, use aggregated data, often focused on activities external to the firm, that may not be particularly accurate. DSSs frequently consist of a model building environment, such as EXCELL, QUATTRO, or 1,2,3, in which the decision support model is constructed and a data management environment used to enter and maintain the data employed in the model. DSSs, in contrast to operational or management control systems, are changed frequently and a key notion behind them is mutual learning about the decision situation by both the analyst and the user (decision maker). Once a DSS is constructed, the rationale behind a decision may be sufficiently understood to permit the system to be converted to an operational or management control system.

Infrastructure consists of the resources that are needed to build a firm's application systems. These resources are hardware, that is, computers, external devices, communications networks; software consisting of operating systems, application building systems, and work environment systems, such as word processors and model building (spread sheets) systems; and staff to build applications, maintain them, and maintain the hardware and software needed to run them. Because of the complexity of the infrastructure and because it must work together (a notion called interoperability), no one organizational unit or project can afford to make major changes. Thus, infrastructure investments tend to be separately funded. Interoperability (see section 28.A.2.b.iii) is one of the more difficult problems in the management of international information systems.

28A.3   FACTORS DRIVING THE USE OF INFORMATION TECHNOLOGY IN MULTINATIONAL FIRMS.   A variety of factors have made the use of information technology (IT) a key ingredient in successful multinational firms. As Hammer (1990) has observed, in the past, the basis for managerial decision making was to minimize cost and to achieve economies of scale in production. He points out that the situation has altered now to where product or service quality, ability to respond quickly to customer needs, and industry changes are as important as cost. Five factors have made the use of IT particularly attractive for international firms.

(a) Global Markets.   With improvements in data communication and international transportation, and with a general lowering of international tariffs, markets have become more global. This tendency becomes more pronounced as regional markets (for example, the EC) develop and with political changes in Eastern Europe. King and Sethi (1992) observe that increases in global trade have been followed closely by rapid growth in service transactions, international monetary transactions and foreign direct investment. In this environment of interdependence, the enhanced role of IT will be a major issue that business executives will face in the future.

In global markets, firms tend to locate production (1) close to the most cost effective labor pool, (2) close to raw materials, or (3) to take advantage of government relations or cultural differences. A key problem for firms operating globally is coordination. IT and particularly data communications can be used to exchange information resulting in improved coordination. For example, Bankers Trust Corporation used an integrated office system to coordinate better the activities of their Asia Pacific Division. With the system, the time to craft and receive approval on financial proposals was reduced on the average from 15 to 3 days.

(b) Need for Flexibility.   IT is altering the relationship among scale, automation, and flexibility. Large-scale production is no longer essential to achieve automation. As a result, entry barriers in a number of industries are falling. After installation of a flexible manufacturing system, BMW can build customized cars, with their own tailored gearbox, transmission, interior, and other features, on the normal assembly line. The increasing flexibility in performing many tasks combined with the falling costs of designing products (often due to the use of computer aided design) has resulted in many opportunities to customize products and serve small market niches.

Because of differences in labor and raw material cost or local government regulation, it is often advantageous for global firms to move operations from a plant in one country to a plant in another. Having a flexible production line facilitates these shifts. When the product is the same throughout the world (e.g., Coca Cola) or is provided by subsidiaries throughout the world (e.g., real estate listings and sales), IT can reduce greatly individual subsidiary costs and foster common quality levels.

(c) Timeliness.   As McFarlan (1992) notes, the required response time for firms operating in the global community is shrinking dramatically. Firms in automobile and construction industries have been able to reduce the design cycle by upwards of 60% through the use of automated design equipment hooked directly to that of suppliers and customers (interorganizational systems—see section 28.A.7.a). McFarlan reports that a $30 million investment in manufacturing and information technology by a UK chemicals company transformed what had been a 10-week order entry and manufacturing cycle down to two days. This permitted the firm to make-to-order.

(d) Concern over Quality.   Led by the Japanese automakers, product and service quality has become a key strategic factor. Maintaining track of faults can permit identification of a part or manufacturing process that requires redesign.

(e) Customer Focus.   Firms that serve traveling customers—airlines, hotels, rental car, and credit card companies—find it necessary to have worldwide customer databases, as do firms that serve customers that demand integrated worldwide service.

(f) Industry Transformations.   Major shifts in industry structure is one of the consequences of this rapidly changing environment. In the late 1970s, McKesson, to compete better with drug store chains, introduced the ECONOMOST order entry and inventory system for their customers, mostly individually owned retail outlets. Cost savings from the system (in terms of lower administrative costs and larger value per order) were passed on to the individual proprietors permitting them to compete more effectively with the chains. Over time, the industry became more concentrated with a number of the chains going out of business (Clemmons and Webber, 1990).

28A.4   CENTRAL CHALLENGES AND STRATEGIES.   Global companies face challenges and follow strategies that are different than those of firms operating within one country.

(a) Challenges.   The challenges of global companies revolve around two basic needs. First is the necessity of resolving differences in culture and to manage effectively headquarters-subsidiary relations. Second is the need to coordinate and control activities globally.

(i) Global versus Local Tensions.   It has rather convincingly been shown that managers in different environments not only have different ways of analyzing and resolving problems but also different information needs on which they base business decisions. This creates a fundamental dilemma for global companies: managers at headquaraters are likely to want different decision information than managers in the local country. Not only this, but the basis for decision making may be fundamentally different. This points out the difficulty of using common systems across a global company.

(ii) Cultural Differences.   A heterogeneous cultural environment makes it more difficult to share common resources. It means products and IT applications require extensive customization. There is some evidence that customers are becoming more alike through the homogenization of needs and desires as a result of communication (e.g., T.V.) and travel and that cultural distinctions are lessening.

Distinctions also exist in styles of systems development. Ives and Javenpaa (1991, p. 45) report,

> . . . that the French were skilled in data modeling and in the more theoretical aspects of systems development. Other interviewees reported the English to be well trained in the use of structured development methodologies, while the Germans were seen as excellent project managers. Singaporeans were described by one interviewee as extremely hard working, skilled, and willing to take on any task assigned. Another manager described them as the consultants of Asia. Australia, on the other hand, was seen as lacking in systems skills.

(iii) Headquarters—Subsidiary Relations.   The primary tension between headquarters and subsidiaries is over control and integration. Subsidiaries desire to act locally—to meet the needs of their local customers. In more general terms, organizations must maintain freedom of action when faced with challenges in their environment. The subsidiary is itself a complex organization and if every action must be cleared with higher level, reaction time is slowed and resources wasted in endless communication. Headquarters, thinking more globally, wants commonality and conformity. For them the challenge is to successfully integrate subsidiaries into the larger organization. This integration becomes more complex as a function of the number of different subsidiaries (breadth) and their scope (diversity).

(iv) Alignment of Business and IT Strategies.   One of the most difficult challenges faced by firms, whether or not operating globally, is the alignment of their IT and business strategies. The goal should be that the IT strategy is consistent with and supports the business strategy. Thus, a multinational firm (see section 28A.4b, ii below) should follow a coordinated global operation strategy (c, i) or a cooperative strategy (c, iii).

(b) Global Business Strategy and IT.   Some business strategies are more dependent than others on timely, accurate, and complete information on overseas operations. There are two broad strategy options for running international operations: country specific and globally integrated.

(i) Country Specific.   When coordination needs are relatively light, home offices often concede considerable autonomy to foreign business. These country specific strategies minimize reporting and information flows between home office and subsidiary. Information technology, under these conditions is primarily used locally and probably decentralized.

(ii) Globally Integrated.   As competition increases and firms search for economies of scale and scope globally, their needs for coordination and control increase. This creates greater demand for information flow between home office and subsidiaries. Bartlett and Ghoshal (1989) identify four broad strategies that an international firm may pursue:

- Multinational, where foreign subsidiaries are operated nearly autonomously or in loose federation so as to sense and respond quickly to diverse local needs and national opportunities.
- Global, where worldwide activities are closely coordinated from headquarters so as to capitalize on economies associated with standardized product design and world-scale manufacturing.
- International that exploits parent company knowledge through worldwide diffusion and adoption.
- Transnational which seeks to retain local flexibility while simultaneously achieving global integration and efficiencies along with worldwide diffusion of innovations. As Bartlett and Ghoshal (1989, p. 69) put it, "dynamic interdependence is the basis of a transnational company—one that can think globally and act locally."

The development of a successful international business over time corresponds to the progression from multinational to transnational strategies. This progression from simple to more complex organization requires increased information for coordination and control and, correspondingly, places greater emphasis on IT.

(c) Global IT Strategies.   Four generic strategies have been identified for the management of IT globally (Ives and Jarvenpaa, 1991).

(i) Independent Global Operations.   Subsidiaries pursue independent system initiatives mirroring the more general multinational strategy of minimum control from headquarters. Technology choices reflect the influence of local vendors as well as prevailing national communication standards and offerings. Technology platforms, databases, and applications are largely non-integrated. The strength of this strategy is local responsiveness. Its weakness is the lack of integration which has the potential to severely impede efforts to implement global business strategies.

(ii) Headquarters Drive.   Headquarters imposes corporate-wide IT solutions on subsidiaries. This is particularly useful for Global firms that strive for worldwide efficiencies. Advantages are that centralized IT provides the coordination and control needed for efficient operations throughout the firm along with some efficiencies of its own. Bringing together headquarters and subsidiary systems staffs may result in some organizational learning. Disadvantages are the clash with local needs and customs, especially if there is not a strong global business push, and the threat of local rejection.

(iii) Cooperative.   Headquarters attempts to influence rather than control the IT choices of their subsidiaries. Personnel are exchanged regularly and joint application development efforts are initiated. Subsidiaries modify applications developed by headquarters. This approach closely parallels the more general international strategy that seeks to rapidly disseminate corporate innovation. Advantages are that systems developed this way are more likely to be adopted, and the organizational learning that results from sharing ideas. Disadvantages are the time and effort required for coordination and the indirect control over outcomes.

(iv) Integrated.   IT applications that reach across national boundaries to meet a firm's diverse objectives. Systems are integrated using international standards and a planned, common IT architecture that meets the needs of various sized organizational units operating in diverse environments. Application modules are divided into common and locally tailored parts. Data entities are shared worldwide and universal data dictionaries and databases are developed. Innovation, in this setting, is a two way street with headquarters benefiting from the knowledge of subsidiaries as well as the reverse. Few companies have reached this level of development.

28A.5   STRATEGIC USE OF INFORMATION TECHNOLOGY.   Since Information Technology (IT) is the primary method for tying together world wide operations, a key issue faced by global firms is their use of IT. However, IT is capable of playing a much more important role than just communications. It can be used for competitive advantage. Several concepts underlie the use of IT for strategic purposes.

(a) Value Chain Analysis.   Porter and Millar (1985) suggest a model of the business firm, called the "value chain," which is useful in recognizing opportunities to apply IT strategically. The value chain divides a company's operations into technologically and economically distinct activities performed in doing business. A business is profitable if the amount buyers are willing to pay for a product or service exceeds the cost of performing the value activities needed to produce it. To gain a competitive advantage over its rivals, a company must either perform these activities at a lower cost, perform a less costly set of activities, or perform them in a way that leads to differentiation and a premium price (i.e., more value).

A firm's value activities fall into nine generic categories (see Exhibit 28A.1). Primary activities, shown on the horizontal axis, are those involved in the physical creation of a product, its marketing and delivery to buyers, and its support and servicing after sales. Activities that allow the primary activities to take place—inputs or infrastructure—that is, support activities, are shown on the vertical axis. Within each of these generic categories, a firm will perform a number of unique activities depending on the particular business.

The value chain for a firm in an industry is embedded in a larger set of activities called the "value system." The value system includes the value chains of suppliers who provide inputs, such as raw materials, to the firm's value chain. The firm's products often pass through the value activities of other firms on their way to the ultimate buyer.

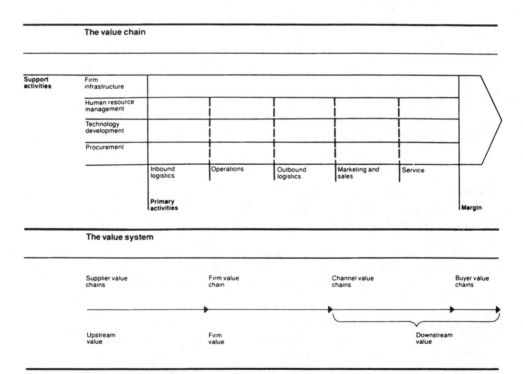

Exhibit 28A.1.   The value chain. *Source:* **Porter, Michael, and Millar, Victor, "How information gives you a competitive advantage,"** *Harvard Business Review,* **July–August 1985, p. 151. Reprinted with permission.**

Firms often differ in competitive scope, or the breadth of their activities. Competitive scope has four dimensions: segment scope (the industry segments in which a firm competes), vertical scope (the degree of vertical integration in a firm), geographic scope, and industry scope (the range of related industries in which the firm competes).

Broad scope can allow a firm to exploit interrelationships between the value chains serving different industry segments, geographic areas, or related industries, for example, by sharing a common sales force. A narrow scope may enable a firm to tailor the value chain of a particular target segment to achieve lower cost or differentiation. The competitive advantage of narrow scope comes from customizing the value chain to serve best particular customers.

(b) Linkages.   The interdependent activities of a firm's value chain are connected by linkages. Linkages exist where the way in which one activity is performed influences the cost or effectiveness of another activity. Linkages often create tradeoffs in performing activities that can lead to competitive advantage. For example, a more extensive product design may lead to reduced after-sale support. To achieve competitive advantage, a company must resolve these tradeoffs consistent with its strategy.

Linkages also require activities to be coordinated. Under these conditions, IT can often play a critical role. Just-in-time delivery of parts requires that inbound logistics, inspection, and operations function together smoothly. Good coordination permits production schedules to be met without the need for costly inventory. Status tracking and good communication of information is at the heart of coordination.

Linkages not only connect value activities inside a company, they create also interdependencies between the firm's value chain and those of its suppliers (firms further upstream) and distributors (firms further downstream). Inspection of external linkages is one of the likely ways to recognize opportunities for competitive advantage. By removing redundant activities and coordinating better those that remain, significant improvement in efficiency can result. For example, a chemical company may save processing steps by persuading its suppliers to deliver compounds in liquid rather than powdered form. As Porter and Millar (1985, p. 150) argue, "careful management of linkages is often a powerful source of competitive advantage because of the difficulty rivals have in perceiving them" and because they permit tradeoffs across organizational boundaries.

"Information technology is permeating the value chain at every point, transforming the way value activities are performed and the nature of linkages among them. It is also affecting competitive scope and reshaping the way products meet buyer needs." (Porter and Millar, 1985, pp. 151–2) This explains why IT has acquired strategic significance and is different from many other technologies businesses use.

(c) Information Content Analysis.   Every activity in the value chain has both a physical and an information processing component. The physical component is more familiar and consists of all of the tasks required to perform the activity. The information processing component consists of the steps required to capture, process, and channel the data necessary to perform the activity.

IT is permitting firms to capture information that was not available before, and it allows more comprehensive analysis of the expanded data. IT is also transforming the physical processing component of activities through the use of computer-controlled machines that are faster, flexible, and more accurate than their manually operated counterparts. IT not only affects how individual activities are performed but, through new information flows, enhances a firm's ability to exploit linkages between activities, both within and outside of firms.

Most products have always had both a physical and an informational component, the latter being everything a buyer needs to know to use the product for the desired purpose and to maintain it. In other words, a product in addition to its physical self, includes information about its characteristics, how it should be used, and supported. For example, convenient accessible information on maintenance and service procedures is an important buyer criterion in consumer appliance.

Historically, a product's physical component has been more important than its informational component. IT, however, makes it feasible to supply far more information, than previously, along with the physical product. Many products process information in their normal functioning. A stereo receiver, for example, often has a mode that allows automatic scanning for strong stations and electronic control of automobile is becoming more visible in dashboard displays.

The trend is towards increasing the information content of the product as well as increasing the information intensity of the value chain used to produce the product. Situations in which both the information content of the product and the information intensity of the value chain are high signal good opportunities to apply IT for competitive advantage.

(d) Transaction Cost Analysis. There are two basic mechanisms for coordinating the flow of materials or services through adjacent steps in the value added chain: markets and hierarchies. Markets coordinate through supply and demand forces, and by external transactions among firms and individuals. Market forces determine the design, price, quantity, quality, and schedule for a given product. The buyer of a good or service has many possible sources and makes a choice based on the best combination of attributes.

Hierarchies coordinate the flow by dictating and controlling it at a higher level in the organization. Managerial decisions rather than the interaction of market forces determine design, quality, cost, and schedule. Thus buyers do not select a supplier from a group of potential suppliers; they simply work with a predetermined one. In many cases the hierarchy is a single firm, although it may be a sole supplier relationship.

Malone et al. (1987) provide a discussion of fundamental tradeoffs between markets and hierarchies in terms of costs for production and coordination. Production costs are those of producing and distributing the goods or services. Coordination costs are the transaction (or governance) costs necessary to coordinate the work of people producing or distributing the goods or services.

In a market with many buyers and sellers, a buyer can compare different sellers and select the one that provides the best combination of characteristics, thus presumably minimizing production costs. The market coordination costs associated with this wide latitude of choice are relatively high because the buyer must gather and process large amounts of information. These costs need also cover additional negotiating or risk covering costs that arise from dealing with "opportunistic" trading partners.

Since hierarchies restrict the buyer's choice of suppliers to one, production costs are, in general higher than the market case due to the absence of competition. The hierarchical arrangement, however, reduces coordination costs by eliminating the buyer's need to gather and process a great deal of information about different suppliers.

Malone et al. (1987) note that two factors qualify these relationships. Products or services that rely on inputs that are highly asset specific will tend to be obtained through the hierarchy rather than the market. An input is asset specific when it can not readily be used by other firms because site, physical, human, or time specificity. For example, a natural resource available at a certain location and movable only at a great cost is site specific. Similarly, products or services that rely on a complex and nonstandard product descriptions will tend to be obtained through the hierarchy rather than the market, because of the difficulty of communicating the details of the product to potential suppliers.

IT has reduced greatly both the cost and time of communicating information. It allows also closer integration of adjacent steps in the value chain through the development of electronic markets and electronic hierarchies. Although this is making both markets and hierarchies more efficient, Malone et al. (1987) argue that these trends will lead to an overall shift toward proportionally more market coordination. Electronic interconnection will lower the per-unit cost of coordination. As markets have a certain production cost advantage over hierarchies, lower coordination costs reduce the importance of these costs and make markets relatively more attractive. In addition, the "electronic brokerage" effect, when many different buyers and suppliers are connected through a central database, lowers further coordination costs. Finally, IT, especially graphics, multi-media, and computer-aided design, will permit more complex product descriptions to be communicated to suppliers and computer-aided flexible manufacturing reducing the importance of asset specificity in many situations, again favoring markets over hierarchies.

28A.6   CHANGING TRADITIONAL INFORMATION FLOWS.   Traditionally, information flows have gone vertically, up the hierarchy, or horizontally among members of a work group, or to subsidiaries, but they have all remained with in the firm's boundaries. When transactions needed to be sent externally hard copy was used, for example, by fax. A new class of systems, interorganizational systems, has emerged that link together, electronically, independent organizational entities These systems have the potential of creating new organizations, altering the structure of industries, and changing the economics of business.

(a) Interorganizational Systems.   SABRE, American Airlines' travel reservation system was started in the late 1960s to manage better American's seat inventory. Specifically, American desired to tie passenger information directly to a seat number on a flight. Because of the size and complexity of the system (heavy data communication combined with a huge transaction volume, a large data base, and high reliability was beyond the technology at the time) it took many years to develop.

Forced by competitor moves to make the system available to travel agents in the mid 1970s, American noted an increase in sales that offset additional costs. American then began to list auto rentals and hotel reservations (that is, the products of other travel related companies) in the system (over time this was replaced with electronic links to the auto company's or hotel's reservation systems, thus making SABRE an interorganizational system) and to list the flights of other airlines (for a fee). When deregulation of the airline industry occurred in the late 1970s, American found themselves in possession of information about passenger demand, which their competitors did not have, that permitted them to structure rates and schedule flights in profitable manner. The airline reservation system is so profitable, that the president of American Airlines said recently, if he had to sell either the reservation system or the airline he would sell the airline.

(b) Electronic Data Interchange.   Electronic Data Interchange (EDI) is the electronic transfer of business information from one independent computer application to another using agreed on standards to structure the data needed to carry out the transaction (Keen, 1992). An example would be a buyer sending a purchase order as an EDI transmission directly into the supplier's order entry (computer) application system. Invoices, delivery notices, bills of lading, and customs declarations can be exchanged in electronic form between computers rather as written communications through the mails The surface advantages are the elimination of paper documents and the clerical steps involved in handling them.

EDI is growing rapidly in Europe and Asia; less so in the USA. This is because with only three time zones and no customs barriers there is less of an incentive than in the remainder of the world. Keen (1992) reports that EDI had doubled the speed of trucks crossing Europe; there is less time waiting at customs and handling paperwork. Hong Kong (Tradelink) and Singapore (TradeNet) have established EDI value-added networks to position their cities in the wider world trading network. Hong Kong has over 100,000 trading firms each sending between 2,000 and 10,000 documents a year. Swire, a typical trading company, has 300 employees, of whom 120 work on documentation, handling nearly one half million bills of lading per year, supported by the same number of shipping papers comprised of 7–8 documents each (Keen, 1992).

(i) EDI Impacts.   The direct impacts of EDI include labor savings in data transcription, control, error investigation and correction; fewer delays in data handling; and reduced time to transmit and process data. These are reflected in improved inventory management, better control of transport and distribution, reduced administrative costs (frequently by a factor of 10 in

per document costs), better cash management, and improved trading partner relations. The indirect benefits of EDI result from a closer integration among related functions within different organizations. As Clark et al. (1992, p. 279) observe, "it is not the replacement of paper by electronic messaging which provides EDI's strategic capabilities, but the associated changes in operation and function within and between organizations which EDI links make possible."

For example, Levi Strauss, through its LeviLink system, has vertically integrated the company's entire apparel manufacturing and marketing cycle (including inventory replenishment, management and reconciliation of purchase orders, receipt of goods, processing and payment of invoices, capture of point-of-sale information, and the analysis of market trends). It is this focus on integration across organizational functions and between firms that distinguishes EDI from other forms of electronic communication (Clark et al., 1992).

Two trends are apparent with EDI: "de-sourcing" and "partnering." De-sourcing refers to the tendency of firms using EDI to reduce the number of suppliers they deal with because of improved reliability that results from better information flows. Partnering is tighter vertical integration (alliances) among corporations.

(ii) EDI Standards.   The standardization of documents (that is, business transactions) was a necessary accompaniment to the replacement of physical transport of paper and magnetic media by electronic transmission. The X12 standard, developed by the American National Standards Institute (ANSI), and the GTDI standard developed in England and Europe are being replaced by the EDIFACT (Electronic Data Interchange for Administration, Commerce and Transport) standard currently under development by a United Nations Joint European and North American (UN-JEDI) working party. Although by the end of 1989 only two documents had been completed (a purchase order and invoice), a full range of business documents will be developed and approved.

28A.7 USING TECHNOLOGY TO CHANGE ORGANIZATION STRUCTURE.   Although there are many ways of organizing workers, a hierarchical structure is most common in the United States. A hierarchy is described by (1) the (average) number of workers reporting to a supervisor (manager) at the next higher level—called "span of control," and (2) number of levels in the organization. Normally, spans of control vary from 4–8 workers reporting to one manager and large organizations may have 3 to 10 levels.

In hierarchies, which have been called "command and control" organizations, directives (or commands) flow from the top to the bottom where they are executed and information flows from the bottom, where it is gathered or generated, to the top. As commands and information move from level to level they become distorted. Drucker (1988) notes that the primary function of middle management is communication—to pass commands down the hierarchy and to transmit information up it to top management where, presumably, decisions are made. By substituting Information Technology (IT) for middle management, accuracy and timeliness of information can be improved, responsiveness increased, and costs reduced.

(a) Knowledge-Based Organizations.   Drucker's (1988) vision for future organizations dealing with knowledge intensive tasks, such as those in consultancies, finance, and publishing, is that they will be structured around small, self organizing groups of professionals. These groups will be highly interconnected by data communications and augmented by various technology based tools which will allow them independence in when and where they work, and to leverage their skills. In these organizations, knowledge will be at the bottom rather than the top, and decisions will be made where the work is performed. Knowledge-based organizations (KBOs) will be much flatter (fewer levels) and leaner than current ones and the role of top management will be to provide culture, and a vision for coordination and synchronization, instead of decision making and direction. Drucker likens KBOs to hospital emergency room teams and string quartets.

(b) Re-engineering Organizations.   Hammer (1990) maintains that businesses are not taking advantage of technology because they tend to follow current procedures when building IT applications rather than rethinking the way work is performed. He notes that the division of labor has gone too far—most workers perform only part of a job and spend needless effort in coordination. Many tasks that are done are unnecessary; they have simply been handed down over time. To cope with this situation, firms should examine their basic business activities so as to recognize those that truly add value. These activities should be retained and others discarded. Organizations and business processes should be redesigned to give workers complete jobs, to capture information once, and to place decision making authority where the work is performed.

28A.8   END-USER COMPUTING.   As mentioned in Appendix A.a.i, due to the high cost and performance attractiveness of mainframe computers, services, up to the early 1980s, tended to be centralized. In that manner, scarce IT resources (equipment and skilled labor) could be more easily shared and fixed costs spread more widely. However, the demand for new and modified applications outstripped the supply of building resources resulting in backlogs for systems development and modification stretching out 2 to 4 years in many firms. This situation was unacceptable.

Information centers (ICs), introduced first by IBM Canada in the early 1980s, provided some relief by making access to data easier. The notion behind an IC is that if (1) terminal equipment, (2) powerful data base query languages, and (3) consulting assistance are made available to users, they could produce their own reports, reducing somewhat the demand for new systems and hence, the backlog.

The second event that changed this situation was the acceptance of the personal computer (PCs) by business (see Appendix A.a.ii). Used first in a stand-alone mode (that is, unconnected to other machines) for individual spreadsheet and database applications, PCs soon became interconnected through Local Area Networks (see Appendix A.b.ii) permitting resources (information and equipment) to be shared and expanding the range of business related activities that could be performed. As more PC application software was developed, the cost of equipment decreased, and performance improved, wide scale diffusion occurred. Professionals performing functional activities, such as lawyers and accountants, became skilled in the application of technology—purchasing packaged software, configuring it to assist them in their work, and sometimes even writing their own programs. This shift in the locus of control and knowledge about computing from centralized support groups to end-users has changed fundamentally the technical power structure in many organizations. Rather than technology being the province of a small elite, it is, today, far more widely distributed.

Consequently, a key issue for management is the effective use and coordination of this distributed technology infrastructure. There is tension between the freedom needed to create innovative applications that have truly beneficial effects, the coordination required for interoperability (which permits resource sharing), and the support (consulting and maintenance) necessary to leverage end-user technology activities.

28A.9   INFORMATION TECHNOLOGY ISSUES FOR GLOBAL MANAGEMENT.

(a) IT Architectures.   One of the difficult questions faced by international managers is how IT architectures should be structured. IT Architecture refers to the configuration and location of information systems hardware and software, data, telecommunications, and IT staffs (see Appendix A.a-b for a detailed discussion of what IT includes). Alavi and Young (1992) note that a firm's IT architecture should be related to its overall strategy (see sections 4.b.i-ii and 4.c). Firms following a country specific or a multinational strategy would have independent local IT facilities at both subsidiary and headquarters locations since these units function relatively independently (this corresponds to the independent Global Operations strategy of section 4.c.ii). Multinational firms often come about through financial investment in a set of existing organizations which then become subsidiaries. Consequently, the technology architecture consists of those developed separately by subsidiaries and headquarters. Additionally, because subsidiaries operate relatively independently, a low level of data integration is needed, with the exception of financial data which is necessary to determine firm performance. Since a relatively small amount of data need to be transferred between headquarters and subsidiaries, direct low capacity data telecommunications links should be sufficient.

Firms following a global strategy with strong central control may well have central IT facilities at headquarters that are shared with subsidiaries along with some local IT support (this corresponds to the Headquarters Drive strategy of section 28A.4.c.ii, although it might also be the Cooperative strategy of section 28A.4.c.iii). Data bases may be firm wide (enterprise wide) and be maintained centrally at headquarters. Since firm wide data needs to be collected globally, the telecommunications architecture would be a vertical hierarchy, with subsidiaries connected to regions where data are aggregated, and regions transmitting aggregated data to headquarters.

A transnational strategy suggests independent coordinated IT facilities at headquarters and subsidiaries (this corresponds to the integrated strategy of section 28A.4.c.iv). Since the strategy is based on rapid firm wide response to local opportunities, information becomes critical. The data architecture would be distributed (but coordinated) with a high degree of connectivity between headquarters and subsidiaries, and among subsidiaries.

Note that as firms evolve and shift their strategies, they may want to change their IT architectures to match better their new approach.

The pressure for interoperability suggests that equipment and software in various categories should be the same throughout a firm. At a minimum careful consideration should be given to how equipment and software in various categories will operate together. For example, if managers at headquarters use Apple Macs, then it is desirable for Macs to be used also at subsidiaries so that managers traveling can use their familiar computer applications. To deal with this issue, many companies adopt standard platforms and software. As a firm operates in more geographic locations, fewer suppliers are able to provide support at all locations. Additionally, a firm operating globally can be faced with high prices for local hardware, lack of local service for products, the absence of an authorized distributor, and long lead times for acquiring equipment and spare parts. Ives and Jarvenpaa (1991) note that establishing locations for international data centers presents challenges of overlapping work hours, local labor regulations, potential theft and sabotage, and unreliable power sources.

(b) Applications.   As firms move toward global and transnational strategies, there is pressure for commonality among application software (see Appendix A.a.iii). It is unlikely that an application system developed at one subsidiary (or headquarters) will meet the needs of other subsidiaries without (1) significant participation from the other subsidiaries and headquarters— both IT staff and functional area representation, and (2) extensive local modification. It takes considerably longer for an information technology project to be completed when the team developing it is from different countries and the resulting software is more complex.

Ives and Jarvenpaa (1991) report that application packages designed to run in one country may be incompatible with their counterparts designed to run in another country. In some countries, local disregard of copyright restrictions have caused vendors to retreat from the market. Due to unavailability, firms may buy packages in one country and then distribute them to subsidiaries in another.

Evolving standards (see Appendix A.b.iii and section 28A.6.b.ii) are the key to worldwide application development. It is essential to adopt a number of standards for hardware, software and communications consistent with the regulatory constraints and supply of technology in different geographic regions.

(c) Communications.   Keen (1992, p. 599) observes that, "International telecommunications is a morass of regulatory, nationalistic and economic complexities." A 500% increase in telecommunications traffic is expected during the 1990s. Telecommunication costs vary widely worldwide and this is becoming a key factor in determining facility location. The fundamental blockage to leveling costs are the PTTs (Poste Telegraphe et Telephonique), the government or quasi-government monopolies for telecommunications. PTTs are naturally unwilling to see their cartel dissolved.

There is some evidence that the quality and reliability of foreign telephone networks is lower than that available in the United States and that effective data transfer speeds are much lower.

(d) Trans-Border Data Flows.   Originally predicted as the trade war of the 1990s, the control of trans-border data has not become a major issue (Ives and Jarvenpaa, 1991). Part of the reason is that many of the laws and regulations governing trans-border data flow (TBDF) are vague and difficult to enforce. The strategy followed by some firms is to inform responsible officials as to what they intend to do and ask if this presents difficulties.

Payroll and personnel records systems, the two classes of applications most vulnerable to TBDF or privacy legislation do not lend themselves to global use. Only the transnational firm may have need for an integrated world wide skills inventory system. Firms need to provide the same level of security and access to personnel data stored abroad as is required by privacy legislation locally.

28A.10   CONCLUSION.   Information Technology (IT) is one of the key factors in the management of international firms. IT permits the better coordination of worldwide operations. IT forms the basis of new products and it has been used to transform industries. International firms that do not invest heavily in an IT infrastructure do so at their risk. IT is no longer a luxury; it is a necessity. In the future the importance of IT to the international firm will only increase.

APPENDIX A: WHAT "TECHNOLOGY" INCLUDES

(a) Computer Technology.   The term "computer" usually refers to what are called general purpose digital computers. General purpose means that the set of instructions (or program) used by the computer to perform a function is stored in the machine's memory and that the program is capable of being changed or modified by the user, thus permitting the computer to be used for multiple purposes simply by replacing the program. This is in contrast to special purpose or dedicated computers where the program cannot be changed by the user. An example of this would be the engine computer that controls spark plug firing and fuel mixture in some automobiles. Digital means that data (and instructions) are represented (within the computer) in binary form.

Computers consist of a central processing unit (CPU) containing a device that decodes and executes instructions, registers (memory) for storing instructions and data while they are being operated on, and input/output channels for communicating with external devices; random access (or main) memory; and external (or peripheral) devices. The CPU operates at a clock (or cycle) rate usually measured in millions of cycles per second (MHertz, abb. MHZ). The faster the clock, the less time it takes to execute an instruction and the faster the computer operates. In today's technology, the CPU may be a single chip operating in the 20–50 MHZ range. The size of random access memory determines the number of instructions or the amount of data that can be operated on without exchange from an external device. The larger random access memory, the less frequently data need be retrieved from an external device and the faster the machine operates since it is much quicker (by more than a factor of four magnitudes) to locate data in main memory than to request it from an external device. External devices consist of storage devices, primarily disk drives, for data storage, printers for producing hard copy output, scanners for data input, and communications devices for data transmission. The latter may permit also the transmission and receipt of FAXes. Other external devices may be VCRs or

Video Disks for multimedia applications, microfilm devices, laboratory equipment just to mention a few.

There are three levels of computer software: operating system, application building, and business applications. The operating system is usually supplied by the computer manufacturer and it makes the resources of the computer available to the program running on the computer (or to the programmer). It is the primary interface to the hardware and consists of memory, data, and job management. Application building software includes programming languages and packages used to build other software. Business applications are programs that perform some specific business activity. They may be purchased and configured or written using application building software.

(i) Mainframe Computers.   These computers are large, fast, and expensive computers with the ability to attach to many devices. From the 1950s through the 1970s the cost-performance of computing favored large computers—if the cost of a computer doubled performance increased more than two times. This led to centralization of computing equipment and computing services, since a large machine was the only effective way to share resources—devices and data. In the mid 1980s, with the advent of the Personal Computer (PC) and Local Area Networks (LANs) this situation began to change. At the present time the cost-performance of computing favors the low end (PC and Workstations) and the high end (massively parallel computers), but disfavors Mainframes in the middle. Mainframes differ from PCs and Workstations mostly in (1) the amount of main memory, (2) the bandwith of their Input/Output channels, (3) the number of devices that can be attached to them, and (4) cost.

(ii) Personal Computers.   These are inexpensive (under $6,000) computers that are fast; have an adequate amount of main memory (up to 10M bytes); a reasonable suite of devices, including hard disk storage (up to 120M byte); and a wide range of application software. PCs have the performance of the Mainframes of ten years ago and the mini-computers of five years ago They are intended primarily for individual use, but the larger ones can support the computing needs of a small business.

(iii) Workstations.   These are fast computers with extensive graphical and communications facilities intended to support computationally intensive tasks such as computer aided design (CAD) or 3-D modeling. Their CPUs tend to be faster than that of a PC and they have more main memory (up to 64M bytes). The price of high end PCs overlap that of low end Workstations. The cost-performance of PCs and Workstations is improving rapidly.

(b) Communications Technology.   Communications technology can be divided into two categories: wide-area networks (WAN) and local-area networks (LAN).

(i) Wide Area Networks.   These are either public utilities, such as ATT Long Lines, or private networks, such as BTNet run by Bankers Trust Corporation. Their purpose is to provide worldwide point-to-point data and voice communication. Public WANs can be divided further into the regular switched telephone network and packet switched digital networks. A local telephone company lays multi-strand cable from your business location to the nearest local switching center. When a call is placed, the telephone number is interpreted at the local switching center and a route is established through the long distance carrier's network to the destination location. Although the telephone network is analog, it is being converted now by telephone companies to digital. Using proper equipment, digital data can be sent over a voice grade normal telephone connection at 19.5 kilo-bits per second (about 2000 characters per second) although 2400 baud (about 200 characters per second) is more common. The advantage of using the public telephone network for digital data transmission is (1) convenience and (2) low cost in that you are charged only for the time the connection is established (plus a

small monthly charge for service) at normal voice telephone rates. The disadvantage is the slow transmission rate.

If a firm desires a greater transmission rate than can be provided from the public telephone network, they can either make use of a switched packet digital network service or they can construct their own private network. To use a switched packet service, a firm would lease a high speed digital line from their business location to the facility of the packet network service provider (usually in the same city). Digital data is then accumulated by the service provider and broken into small (that is, 4000 character) packets and transmitted over the packet network to the city of the recipient where it is distributed to the recipient over another leased line (these lines are often microwave links). To construct a private digital network, a firm would lease lines (and probably some equipment) from the telephone companies at set tariffs.

The advantage of using a packet network service for transmitting moderate amounts of data at high speed is cost—other than the leased lines, charges are on a per-use basis. That is, you pay only for the number of packets transmitted independent of distance traveled. In order to use a packet network, both the sender and the recipient must have access to the network. A private network, on the other hand, may be cost effective on a per unit of data basis if a sufficiently large amount of data is transmitted to cover the line and equipment charges.

(ii) Local Area Networks. The purpose of a Local Area Network (LAN) is to interconnect workers in a relatively homogeneous work area (a department) and connect them to various resources. It is the way that information is distributed to end users and how they obtain computing, printing, and data resources. There are two basic LAN architectures: ethernet and token ring.

With ethernet, each device has their own address and is connected to a buss, terminated at its end, with a cable and an interface card (in the device). A device wishing to transmit data to another device looks at the buss to see if it is busy. If it is not it puts its data packet, with the address of the destination device in the beginning, on the buss as a series of digital characters. All devices on the buss look to see if the transmission is for them (that is, has their address). If so they read the data; if not, they ignore it. The difficulty with an ethernet architecture is that collisions occur when two devices put data on the buss simultaneously. When this occurs the data is lost and both packets must be retransmitted. As the amount of data on the buss increases, so does the likelihood of collisions. Thus, the performance of ethernet LANs degrade rapidly as data rate increases. Ethernets function effectively up to about 2–5 million characters per second (and this limit is being constantly improved).

The beginning and end of a token ring LAN are connected together in a ring (or circle). Each device, which has its own address is connected to the token ring with a cable and interface card (located in the device). When a device wishes to transmit data to another device, it waits for the trolley (a special control packet) to come around the ring. If the trolley does not have another device's token in it, the device places its token in the trolley and transmits its data packet. Devices on the ring look at each data packet to see if it is for them. If so they read it; if not they disregard it. The advantage of a token ring architecture is that performance degrades less rapidly as a function of load because collisions and retransmission of data are avoided. The disadvantage is that token rings are more expensive because the interface card is more complicated than the one for ethernet and there is extra control circuitry. Token ring LANs function in the 4–8 million character per second range (and their performance, too, is improving).

LANs can be connected together by devices called routers and hubs permitting data to be transferred among them. They may also be connected to Wide Area Networks (WANs), through gateways, forming hierarchies of data networks.

Two notions are helpful in order to understand the potential of LANs: resource sharing and connectivity. It is common on a LAN to dedicate one computer as a file server which runs the LAN operating system and maintains shared data files. Thus, computers connected to the LAN can share programs; they need not all have copies of their own programs. This simplifies greatly program maintenance as only one program need be updated. In a similar manner one computer is often designated as a print server allowing one printer to be shared among many users. Connectivity refers to the ability to send messages and other forms of data to the members of a work group. In highly connected work groups (1) people with particular expertise can be shared, and (2) constraints of working together in time and space can be relaxed. That is, high connectivity permits asynchronous messages to be sent across a wide geographic area. Applications software that facilitates coordination among workers is called "groupware" (see section 28A.10.e).

LANs do add another level of complexity beyond stand alone computers and it often is necessary to allocate part of a person's time to troubleshooting and providing assistance to other workers.

(iii) Data Interchange Standards.   There are two types of data interchange standards: proprietary and internationally recognized. Proprietary standards are protocols developed by one company for use among their product line and customers. For example, IBM's System Network Architecture (SNA) is a proprietary communications protocol. Proprietary standards may become defacto if they are adopted by a majority of the firms and customers in a field.

Internationally recognized standards are developed by committees representing various interest groups. In data communications, the International Standards Organization (ISO) has developed seven layer data communications architecture that is widely followed. X400 is a service protocol for the exchange of electronic mail among different systems and X500 is a directory and naming protocol (under development) that run at the ISO application layer. X25 and TCP/IP are lower level protocols running at the ISO transport and network layers. The importance of adhering to international standards is that they increase the chance of interoperability among equipment. The difficulty with international standards is that they take a long time to develop and to be approved (10 years is not unusual) and even longer before products that conform to them are released.

APPENDIX B: TRENDS IN TECHNOLOGY FOR GLOBAL MANAGEMENT

(a) Economics of Technology.   For a constant cost, the performance of technology doubles approximately every two years. This trend is likely to continue for the foreseeable future. For a discussion of the relative cost and performance of mainframes, PCs, and workstations see section 28A.2.a.i-iii.

(b) Open Systems.   Many operating systems (see section 2.a) provided by computer manufacturers are proprietary. Proprietary operating systems (1) limit the selection of equipment that can run the operating system to that of one manufacturer and (2) cost relatively more than "open" operating systems. Since the goal of many IT managers is to be able to use hardware that has the best cost performance, it is advantageous not to be locked into the products of one manufacturer. An open operating system is one available for computers manufactured by many companies. Today, UNIX is the primary open operating system.

(c) Distributed Architectures.   Most application systems are designed to run on one computer system. With the advent of Local Area Networks (see section 28A.2.b.ii) and End-User Computing (section 28.A.9), highly interconnected networks of smaller computers have emerged. Distributed architectures permit an application system to be divided such that a portion of it runs locally on the user's Workstation or PC (see section 28A.2.a.ii-iii) and a portion runs remotely on computers elsewhere on the network. One popular architecture for distributed processing is the Client/Server model where client software requests services from server software and clients and servers may be running on different computers. The Open

Software Federation's (OSF) Distributed Processing Environment (DPE) and Distributed Management Environment (DME) are intriguing distributed architectures.

(d) Multimedia.   Multimedia systems are integrated text, graphics, video, and audio subsystems in a single workstation. Today, video is provided by a read only video disk player and a special video adapter card. In the future video will be available from CDs and eventually from digital data stored on external disk memory (see section 28A.2.a). Authoring software permits editing of video data, the creation of hyper-media links, text editing, and graphics creation. The primary application of multimedia systems is in education, training, and promotion where they have the potential of making these activities more interesting and realistic.

(e) Computer Supported Cooperative Work.   Most computer application software is designed to support a single user. However, almost all business activity takes place in work groups. Computer Supported Cooperative Work (CSCW) software or (Groupware) is designed to support more than one person in either synchronous (for example, group decision making) or asynchronous (for example, co-authoring systems or smart electronic mail filters) activities. While these systems are still mostly experimental, Lotus Notes has emerged as application building system many firms are using. CSCW applications are exciting because they give promise of skill augmentation that could be useful in Knowledge-Based Organizations (see section 8.a).

SOURCES AND SUGGESTED REFERENCES

Maryam Alavi and Greggry Young. "Information technology in an international enterprise: An organizing framework," in *The Global Issues of Information Technology Management,* Sjailendra Paluia, Prashant Paluia, and Ronald Zigli, eds., Harrisburg, PA: Idea Publishing, 1992.

ANSI X12. "An introduction to Electronic Data Interchange," ANSI X12 Data Interchange Standards Association, Suite 355, 1800 Diagonal Road, Alexandra, VA 22314, USA.

C.A. Bartlett and S. Ghoshal. *Managing Across Borders: The Transnational Solution,* Boston, MA: Harvard Business School Press, 1989.

Roger Clark, P. DeLuca, J. Gricar, T. Imai, D. McCubbrey and P. Swatman. "The international significance of Electronic Data Interchange," in *The Global Issues of Information Technology Management,* Sjailendra Paluia, Prashant Paluia, and Ronald Zigli, eds., Harrisburg, PA: Idea Publishing, 1992.

Eric Clemmons and Michael Row. "McKesson Drug Company." *MIS Quarterly,* 5, 1, 1988.

Peter Drucker. "The Coming of the New Organization." *Harvard Business Review,* Jan./Feb. 1988.

Michael Hammer. "Reengineering Work." *Harvard Business Review,* July/August 1990.

Blake Ives and Sirkka Jarvenpaa. "Applications of Global Information Technology: Key Issues for Management." *MIS Quarterly,* March, 1991, pp. 33–49.

————. "Planning Globally: Practical Strategies for Information Technologies in the Transnational Firm," in *The Global Issues of Information Technology Management.* Sajailendra Paluia, Prashant Paluia, and Ronald Zigli, eds., Harrisburg, PA: Idea Publishing, 1992.

William King and Vikram Sethi. "A framework for Transnational Systems." in *The Global Issues of Information Technology Management,* Sjailendra Paluia, Prashant Paluia, and Ronald Zigli, eds., Harrisburg, PA: Idea Publishing, 1992.

Thomas Malone, Joanne Yates, and Robert Benjamin. "Electronic Markets and Electronic Hierarchies." *Comm. ACM, 30,* 6, (June) 1987, pp. 484–497.

Warren McFarlan. "Multinational CIO Challenge for the 1990s," in *The Global Issues of Information Technology Management.* Sjailendra Paluia, Prashant Paluia, and Ronald Zigli, eds., Harrisburg, PA: Idea Publishing, 1992.

Michael Porter and Victor Millar. "How Information Gives You a Competitive Advantage." *Harvard Business Review,* July–August, 1985, pp. 149–160.

Edward Roach. *Managing Information Technology in Multinational Corporations.* New York: MacMillan, 1992.

CHAPTER 29

INTERNATIONAL TRANSFER PRICING

Finbarr Bradley

Dublin City University

SUPPLEMENT CONTENTS

29.2 OBJECTIVES AND POLICIES.

Page 29 • 4, replace Taxes (10%/10%) with Taxes (10%/50%) in Low-Markup Policy half of Table.

Page 29 • 5, replace Taxes (10%/10%) with Taxes (10%/50%) in Low-Markup Policy half of Table.

29.6 U.S. TRANSFER PRICING PROPOSALS.

Page 29 • 27, replace subsection (e) Advanced Determination Rulings *with:*

(e) Advance Pricing Agreements (New).   Under the Advance Pricing Agreement Program drawn up in 1991, the IRS is urging companies to apply voluntarily for price determinations in advance. These would allow companies to guarantee that a proposed transfer pricing policy was acceptable to the IRS and therefore help avoid a possible audit. There is, understandably, some reluctance on the part of companies to apply for such agreements. One reason is that detailed economic analysis would be required involving the gathering of extensive data. Another reason is Sections 6110 and 6103 of the Internal Revenue Code, which deal with public disclosure of prior written determinations. Some companies fear that, by exposing themselves, competitors may be able to gain access to confidential financial and competitive information.

29.7A RECENT PROPOSED SECTION 482 REGULATIONS (NEW).

Page 29 • 28, add new section:

In January 1992, the IRS proposed new U.S. Section 482 regulations. While these proposals contain some of the same modifications to existing regulations contained in the 1988 White Paper, many controversial proposals have now been dropped. Lederman and Hirsh (1992) examine in detail the ramifications of the proposed regulations. Essentially, the proposals adopt a similar methodological approach for the pricing of transfers of intangibles and the pricing of sales of tangible property. First priority will now be given to pricing based on comparable uncontrolled transactions, referred to as the "matching transaction" method with respect to intangibles and the "comparable uncontrolled price" method (CUP) with respect to tangibles. The new priority is given to pricing under the "comparable adjustable transaction" method (CAT) for intangibles and the cost plus or resale price methods for tangibles. Permission to use these second priority methods will only be given if the resulting reported operating income falls within a "comparable profit interval." If the reported operating income does not fall within this interval, then the "comparable profit" method may be used for tangibles, but only if the reported operating income falls within the comparable profit interval. With respect to cost-sharing arrangements, the proposals impose additional conditions upon those of the present regulations. A key new condition is the requirement that the participants make continuing efforts to measure the share of benefits that each expects to receive from the developed intangibles, as such projected benefits evolve over the term of the agreement, and to divide the costs accordingly.

Lederman and Hirsh (1992) believe that the biggest beneficiary of the proposed Section 482 regulations will be the Advance Pricing Agreement program since it may encourage more multinationals, both U.S. and non-U.S., to utilize this program to reduce the potential for controversy left by the proposed regulations.

SOURCES AND SUGGESTED REFERENCES

Page 29 · 29, add the following:

A. S. Lederman and B. Hirsh. "Proposed Section 482 Regs. Adopt Comparable Profit Interval Requirement." *Taxes*, April 1992.

CHAPTER 30

INTERNATIONAL TAXATION

Paul M. Bodner

Deloitte & Touche

SUPPLEMENT CONTENTS

30.2 OVERVIEW.

Page 30 · 3, add at end of fourth line:

corporate

30.3 U.S. TAXATION OF A FOREIGN OPERATION.

Page 30 · 5, delete, at end of line 13:

and South Africa

Page 30 · 8, delete, at end of line 9:

and South Africa

30.5 TRANSFER—PRICING.

Page 30 · 15, add to item (b) Specific Transactions:

On January 24, 1992, the Internal Revenue Service proposed comprehensive regulations stating its position relative to the transfer of intangible and tangible property. These regulations are extremely complex and controversial. It is anticipated that they will be modified before they are finally adopted.

30.6 FOREIGN CURRENCY ISSUES.

Page 30 · 18, add to end of item (d):

The IRS has proposed regulations that will require a QBU whose functional currency is a hyperinflationary currency, to use the "dollar approximate separate transactions" method of accounting.

SUPPLEMENT INDEX